FRANCO'S BASTARD
LOLA BRECHT

Sketch of Dic Edwards by Anthony Unsworth

Dic Edwards

FRANCO'S BASTARD
LOLA BRECHT

Introduction by Dic Edwards
and Torben Betts

OBERON BOOKS
LONDON

First published in 2002 by Oberon Books Ltd.
(incorporating Absolute Classics)
521 Caledonian Road, London N7 9RH
Tel: 020 7607 3637 / Fax: 020 7607 3629
e-mail: oberon.books@btinternet.com

A catalogue record for this book is available from the British Library.

ISBN: 1 84002 306 6

Cover design: Andrzej Klimowski

Typography: Jeff Willis

Sketch of Dic Edwards by Anthony Unsworth

Printed in Great Britain by Antony Rowe Ltd, Chippenham.

Contents

A special thanks to Jeni Williams
and to Torben Betts for his commitment to this book
Thanks to Edward Bond for the constancy of his support
Thanks to James Hogan and Charles Glanville
Thanks to Amanda for the typing
and Bunny for our shared West Wales history

Introduction

Dic Edwards talks to the playwright Torben Betts

TB: Given that your work has largely been repudiated by our national companies, what do you think it is about your particular style of theatre that sits so uneasily with the UK's literary departments?

DE: I'm not sure. The first thing I always think is that the work is just not good enough. 'Repudiated' suggests that someone has sat down somewhere and said: 'We will repudiate Edwards.' I think that mostly they just haven't noticed me, though in the Eighties when I started out, successive literary managers at both the Royal Court and The Bush wanted to do my work. In the case of the Court – where I actually had a writer's pass – the artistic director didn't like me (on a personal level) and vetoed any attempt to get my work produced there.

What I'd like to believe is that today's mainstream British theatre wants entertainments merely. I think most of my plays are entertaining but often in difficult ways. Most obviously in the sense that they make you think. But I do seriously believe that mainstream theatre is to be found in the work of a writer like Bond – who really has been repudiated – while in the whole history of theatre, current West End and 'mainstream' theatre will be seen itself as being the fringe.

TB: You've spoken before about your opposition to what you term 'the theatre of representation', which is clearly the language of television. It seems that a serious playwright that wants to survive in any way at all must nowadays either develop a second profession or succumb to the inevitable and write for TV, generally losing both freedom and control in the process. How is theatre to be saved from the demands for accessibility, easy answers and broad audience appeal? Why, because a writer is deemed 'difficult', should his/her work be overlooked?

DE: The problem with theatre is that it seems to have lost sight of its purpose. Go back to the beginning in Greece (in Western theatre) and you will find a theatre that concerned itself with society. If Aristotle was right that man is a political animal (by which I think he means that man has the intelligence that denies him, ultimately, ignorance and the failure to recognise other people, and so he cannot live alone but has to live in society), then there is a responsibility on the guardians of intelligence to exercise vigilance in the monitoring of social structures. The guardians of intelligence are all those who have a desire for establishing truths. These include (ought to include) philosophers, writers, artists and, perhaps, teachers. It's their role within democracy. They are up against lawyers and politicians (certainly in our society) who manipulate truths for a different end. If the operation of the mechanics of society is left to the lawyers and politicians unopposed then democracy is diminished. Where is this opposition to be staged? Not in parliament or in council chambers because there is the tacit assumption that because the people who populate these arenas are elected they are somehow delegated to speak for us so our subsequent speaking to them is made redundant! This, of course, is the central flaw of representational democracy. We need another arena.

It may be felt that TV is that arena and that programmes like *Panorama* and *Newsnight* fulfil this monitoring function. The problem with this is the relationship between the audience and the screen. I've said elsewhere that the space between the audience and any screen is a dead space which renders the experience of the audience a passive one so I don't want to go into it here. But it means that the audience has to rely on the intelligence and determined application of that intelligence by the TV presenter to discover the truth about the story – assuming that that story is the necessary one! So while these programmes are useful, they don't work. The thing that's missing is the moral involvement of the audience; the audience's own creativity and the presentation of the story in a way that engages these two elements. Even *Question Time* and programmes like it which seem to be interactive and are occasionally quite splendidly theatrical, fail because they have no sense of story.

We still have the philosophers, artists and teachers. Teachers are constrained by the National Curriculum and so are ineffective. Philosophers – as I tried to show in *Wittgenstein's Daughter* – have abandoned truth and arrived at the end of history (not to mention philosophy itself) and the effectiveness of much of the art world as part of that debate (here at least) is determined by Saatchi and Saatchi so that we have most of our new artists playing silly games in a twilight world of fascist modernism that should have died with the last century.

This leaves the theatre and its playwrights! Theatre is the only place where you can tell the necessary story of our social lives in a way which actively and creatively and morally engages the audience and their intelligence and in a way that satisfies democracy's desire for opposition to the lawyers and other constrainers of truth.

Of course, theatre has been almost entirely taken over by what I call unfashionably the bourgeois class and that class has no interest in discovering the truths about our society and bellicose capitalism because they profit from it! They just want to be entertained. This has determined that the theatre has become a place of spectacle which involves the spectacle of actually arriving at the building as much as the spectacle of, say, people *acting!* As television is naturally inclined to entertain through its reproduction of real life so that the audience may, say, get a vicarious pleasure at the suffering of others but no intellectual stimulation, then a confusion has built up over the relationship between TV and theatre which can lead seriously regarded commentators (as I saw recently) to argue that our new theatre writers should learn from those writing for TV!

The answer for writers writing for the theatre is to recognise that if you write your plays like TV shows then ultimately people will stop going to the theatre to see anything other than the most spectacular musicals because they can get what you're offering on TV. And, of course, there's the sense of responsibility that every artist has to his/her art and what those responsibilities are in your own case.

TB: So the passivity of watching TV and cinema is due to the fact that they merely describe events and situations, whereas theatre asks why these things should be as they are. Would you say that the simple fact of being present at a live event makes very real demands upon the moral sense of the spectator, demands which are not made in any other form of drama?

DE: If I can make the distinction by concentrating on cinema and theatre, I think it's like this: in cinema the writer is relatively unimportant. This is because a film tells its stories in pictures and the person most responsible for how those pictures look is the director. And just because of this – because of the director's ultimate authority over what ends up on the screen – the audience will only ever see what the director wants it to see. This is an extremely profound reality because the director doesn't only determine *what* you see but *how* you see it. In other words, using close-ups, say, or emotionally charged music etc. In this way he can manipulate the audience's intellectual/emotional responses. It's this that renders the audience passive because they have no creative role (beyond either liking or disliking a film). And because they have no creative role they have no moral connection in the sense that they need to make decisions about what's going on. Of course, you may say that you respond to the film in spite of the director's intention which means you have some kind of role and are part of a decision-making process. But you can't escape the fact that the director has dictated the terms.

In theatre it's the writer who is most important. The director shouldn't be important at all other than in an organisational sense. The director's importance is in the planning of rehearsals and in his/her determination to get the actors to understand the play fully. Once directors begin to *direct* they encourage actors to *act* and what you get is both directors and actors dictating to the audience the meaning of the play. And so the writer has a responsibility to write his play in a way that leaves the audience having to decide the issues of the play. Nothing in the writing should direct the audience to think one thing or another. This works: a woman I know went to see *Wittgenstein's Daughter* and was very taken with it and even excited because she thought it was an anti-gay play – and about time too. Of course it's nothing of the sort but it got this debate out of her. I would argue that her response was not passive but creative and moral.

I do believe that being in the audience at a play (not, I should say, a play in a large, modern proscenium arch theatre where it's difficult to connect audience with stage) involves one in something unique. The very fact that actors are live human being means that the space between the 'stage' and the audience is fraught with a kind of intellectual tension which becomes the battlefield of ideas.

TB: What about the language, the poetry of your work? Your plays exist very much in a world of their own and with a language very much their own, often bestowing upon the dispossessed and oppressed characters who drive the work a powerful blend of rage and eloquence. It's impossible to confuse the language of these worlds with that inhabited by the audience member. Would you say this is essential to eradicate the recognition factor that so much of our drama relies upon?

DE: I think you're talking about dramatic language. Dramatic language serves the dramatic purpose of the play. I think dramatic context is poetic. I also think that the genre that theatre is most like is poetry, with its concentration of idea, imagery and purpose. So it seems natural that the more passionate the playwright is about his/her subject, the more poetic he/she will become.

Another distinction, I think, between film/TV and theatre is that the former tells its story with pictures, the latter with words. (I think I heard Mamet say this.) In film and TV language is used very much in the service of the plot. So the characters need to say what needs to be said in order to get the plot to go where you want it to. Of course it's not as simple as that in the post-Tarantino cinema but let's say it's what you can get away with. Language in theatre has a very different function. It serves the dramatic purpose. Also, I think my theatre deals a lot with appearance and reality (obviously) and I believe that there are languages which relate to these: the language of appearance and the language of reality. I think one of the ways we create dramatic tension is to have a conflict between the two – if you like, between what people *seem* to need to say and what they *actually* need to say. I think my 'oppressed' characters are more likely to say what they *need* to say while the oppressor characters say what they *seem* to need to say: by which I mean what they need to say in order to keep their authoritarian positions.

TB: I would describe you very much as a tragedian: your work is highly poetic and theatrical, is conceived on an epic scale, features characters who do the wrong things but perhaps for the right reasons, and who, with both intensity and wit, struggle against the forces which oppress them. You might not agree with this definition but do you see yourself as a writer of tragedies?

DE: Tragedy strictly speaking, I suppose, is the fall of great people (*peripeteia*), a fall conceived by the gods and aided by their own tragic flaws. I suppose we can have some sympathy with them because what happens to them is not entirely of their own making. It's inconceivable to me that today we wouldn't expect our main characters to be responsible for their own wickedness etc. So I have replaced the tragic flaw with *stupidity* and it's the common man who's tragic and his tragedy is self-induced, brought on by stupidity. The stupidity itself is encouraged by the pettiness of small personal advantage that people pursue at the expense of the wider reading of their lives and the context of their lives. Of course, all of us at some time are stupid, which means that we can sympathise if not empathise with the characters and the tragedies of the small common man then become a passion for us all.

TB: This question of sympathy is a central issue in drama; *But I just didn't care about any of these people!* is a common complaint. In *Franco's Bastard*, where the central character is a violent psychopath, a rapist, a racist and a fascist, you manage to make Carlo, through both the strength of his personality and his use of language, seductive rather than sympathetic. Consequently you make his story compelling. The co-existence of these forces of repulsion and attraction creates an anxiety in the audience which is creative. Do you set out to do this consciously or is it simply your instinct as a playwright?

DE: I wouldn't want to mislead you with my last answer into too simple an understanding of what I meant by 'sympathise'. My characters are the means by which I convey the arguments of my play. I would much prefer to think that the audience were sympathising with the arguments, by which I must mean connecting with them at an intellectual level.

Recently I had an argument with a director about the end of a play I'd just written – which was, it has to be said, based on a misunderstanding. I thought he was saying that the end is no good because things are too resolved and you need the audience to go away and wonder what might have happened afterwards. I said (misunderstanding him): 'No, the action must always be resolved. What we want them to be thinking about after the play is the arguments.' It's the arguments that must be unresolved: this is how you connect the audience with the play on a moral and creative level.

I hope Carlo in *Franco's Bastard* is seductive because then we might get the audience sympathising with a character who's actually a fascist, which ought to make them wonder about where they stand politically. So I do set out to achieve the effect you've summarised in your question.

TB: You subtitle the play 'a Welsh Pastoral', it being partly a meditation on the state of the Welsh nation. What exactly do you mean by 'pastoral' here and what was the inspiration behind using an illegitimate son of the Spanish dictator to drive the play?

DE: In a sense it is a meditation on Wales but I'd like to think it has universal application. In another way it's a contemplation on the relationship between city and country: the differences are magnified in Wales because the cities – most notably Cardiff, have English-language cultures while the rural areas of the West and North are predominantly Welsh-speaking and the culture is different. So the use of 'pastoral' is intended to draw attention to this dichotomy, but also I'm using it ironically in the sense that one thinks of something pastoral as something peaceful – while in the play the pastoral harbours violence and hatred.

Finally, the person I was thinking about when I wrote the play – he was the head of a quasi-terrorist organisation called the Free Wales Army– actually had a Spanish mother. I was actually attacked one night by him and a henchman with a bottle and hammer. Between them they broke my jaw and put me in hospital for a week. Strangely, there was something amateur about it and it occurred to me that there would be something amateurish about this person thinking he may actually be the son of Franco and quite funny, I think, that he might think this and regard himself, as a consequence, as a bastard!

TB: When Ben tells Sion how he killed a man with the frozen salmon, he asks if Carlo is 'a man who would recognise the gut anger and loneliness of one who feels abandoned, evicted within his own country.' It strikes me that this theme of eviction is the lifeblood that runs through your work in general.

DE: The literary cultural establishment of Wales is Welsh language. So if you're not a part of that it's as if you don't exist. This is why so little of Welsh writing gets to the outside world – apparently, in Richard Eyre's book *Changing Stages* while there's obviously a huge section on English Theatre, a very big one on Irish and a substantial one on Scottish Theatre, there's not one *sentence* on Welsh Theatre!

Welsh language culture is content to speak to itself – and it gets huge subsidies, rightly or wrongly, to do so – so there's nothing here pushing the English language work out – though the company doing *Franco's Bastard* are hoping to take it to London. I compare this experience for English-language Welsh writers to being left to sleep on the street outside your own home.

But of course 'eviction' is not just this. Many writers don't fit into bourgeois culture and so are evicted in that sense too.

TB: Other major themes in your work are the relationship between sexual repression and political suppression (notably in *Casanova Undone*) and the sense that characters are operating in worlds that are very much 'at the end of history' (*Wittgenstein's Daughter*). You combine these concepts in *Lola Brecht* as you survey the psychological landscape from which so much of Europe's barbarity has sprung. Would you say that Lola is an extension and development of your other heroines (for example, Alma in *Wittgenstein's Daughter* and Regan in *Regan*) in that she struggles to reclaim her own voice, her own language and finally to take control of her own destiny? How did this extraordinary play come into being?

DE: Lola reminds me a lot of Sylvia in *Looking For The World*. Like that character, her language and the truths that she would convey through it are sat upon by a fat-headed husband who's only really interested in his version of the world. But also, like Alma, I think you'll gather that my women characters are much more the truthseekers than the men who are often stupid for the reasons I've suggested elsewhere.

Lola Brecht was written first as a play simply called *Lola* which had a rehearsed reading in Cardiff in 1985. It dealt with a woman on her honeymoon trapped with her husband in a hotel (he is as much her imprisoner) while race riots are taking place in the street. A concierge tries to seduce her. I can't remember much more than that about it except that Rob Ritchie when he was Literary Manager at the Court really tried to get it on there and when he failed did his best with Hampstead. I don't have a copy of it now. Anyway, a local amateur/semi-professional company said they could give me £500 if I could come up with something. It was the time of the Bosnian conflict. I had been commissioned to write a play for Theatr Clwyd by the then artistic director Helena Kaut-Howson. I wrote my version of Dostoievsky's *The Idiot* (also the title of my play) dealing with the Bosnian conflict and she got sacked and so it wasn't going to be done. At about the same time I read about Rheinardt Bonnke the German evangelist and the absurdity of everything seemed to take shape for me so I took the old *Lola* play which was already quite absurd and quite quickly wrote about the Brechts. It was one of those works which you write when the time feels absolutely right – with an urgency, and throwing in everything you've got stored. It's a bit like Dylan's *Hard Rain's A'Gonna Fall*. I read how he wrote that at the time of the Cuban missile crisis when he felt there may be only a matter of days left and no time to be too particular. So every unsaid line he had he used. *The Idiot* has never been produced.

TB: Your plays are notable for their theatricality and use of traditional devices which have now all but died out: the long soliloquy, the aside to the audience, the eavesdropper and, in *Lola Brecht*, the use of the almost Jacobean cross-dressing device of Imra and Imri (a kind of throwback to the Sophie/Costa character in *Casanova Undone*). What has drawn you to these techniques over the years?

DE: These devices have died out, I think, because they are so theatrical. So many playwrights these days, I suppose, are influenced by film and TV and these devices don't work in the same way in those media. But I love comedies of errors! Because it's not simply mistaken identity, it's about people believing what they want to believe (as with Paddy in *Looking For The World* who wants to believe he's on a holiday island when, in fact, he's on a prison island!). I repeat: theatre should tell its story metaphorically. The thing about *Lola Brecht* is that, really, it couldn't possibly happen (like *Wittgenstein's Daughter* with its ghost of the dead philosopher), but if we follow Coleridge's advice and suspend our disbelief, what we see on stage is more real than what we appear to see in 'reality'. The wonderful thing about *the play* is that it can be playful! And there's nothing more playful than mistaken identity which carries the weight of the appearance/reality dichotomy at a much deeper level. This is the *noumenal* quality of theatre. And there is the playfulness between the levels of reality.

The kind of theatre I dislike most is the kitchen sink stuff that was around in the Sixties and, I think, is back again. People think it's working-class theatre but it's not. It's middle-class theatre. It's condescending. It's middle-class writers making themselves feel better by creating caring pictures of working-class difficulties. True working-class theatre wants to make the middle class feel worse by analysing the culture that they manage which has evicted me and my class. The best example of this is New Labour: a middle-class ethos took over a working-class party with its core vote then kicked out the working-class values thus leaving that core vote, which has nowhere else to go, evicted. Also, of course, it's government by lawyers – there should be a name for it: *legalocracy* or something. My play *Black September,* which deals with the life of the French poet Baudelaire, is about this.

Western politics uses language to deny democracy (from Nazi propaganda to New Labour's sound bites); theatre should use language to promote it. Another of my plays, *Low People*, is about this. Theatre should be in direct conflict with the political system. That conflict should centre on language.

The purpose of language now is to win elections and to entertain. This purpose has so dislocated us from the truth that most people don't vote. This is not alarming to politicians even though they say it is. It means that the other function of language – to entertain – is working. Everything now, including most theatre, is show biz. The idea is to entertain the people to the extent that nothing else means anything and they become entirely passive. Then they are controlled and politics can be left to the political classes.

Dic Edwards and Torben Betts
January–April 2002

FRANCO'S BASTARD
a Welsh Pastoral

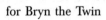

for Bryn the Twin

Characters

CARLO FRANCISCO FRANCO LLOYD HUGHES
forties

SERENA/RUBY
twenties

BEN
twenties

SION
twenties

The set is the space. On the floor of the stage there is a large Welsh flag as though a mosaic on the floor of Carlo's home in West Wales. There is a large table centrally and at back a record-player.

Franco's Bastard was first performed at Chapter Arts Centre, Cardiff, by Sgript Cymru on 10 April 2002 with the following cast:

CARLO, James Coombes

SERENA/RUBY, Karin Diamond

BEN, Adam Randall

SION, Shane Attwooll

Director, Simon Harris

Designer, Max Jones

Lighting Designer, Elanor Higgins

PART ONE

Scene 1

A fishmonger's yard. Cardiff. One Winter morning.

BEN is standing looking at audience. He speaks above the heads of the audience as though to someone physically above him. He is speaking through his tears.

BEN: When I broke down in Caerphilly...no, it wasn't my fault...IT WASN'T! the...u...the...the bloody clutch went! And when I broke down in Caerphilly and I couldn't get up the hill and you sent out that bastard in the VW...I was...he was pulling me down Thorn Hill...I was like a like a...u...well, you've got a choice: I was like a balloon on a string or a piece of fish bait on a pater noster! I mean, that truck I was driving wasn't meant to go seventy miles an hour! I mean...I could have rolled the bastard thing! (*Pause.*) You stole my money! You stole my mon... (*Short pause.*) How'd you mean it was YOUR money? I earned it! It was your money before you gave it to me but once I EARNED it it was MY money! And...and...and...well I gave it back!...I gave it back to you because I trusted you to...okay. Let's go through this. Right? Okay. Let's go through this: it's Easter. This is Easter. It's a holiday. Okay? And at Easter we get a bonus. Okay? This is right isn't it? We get a bonus. So I'm calculating: I've done my week's work and my wage was, say, 140 quid. Right? And then the bonus which is related to the number of weeks I've worked since the last bonus I figure ought to come out at about another 120 quid. Okay. So when I'm picking up my wages I'm expecting to get 260 quid. But when I pick up the packet there's only 120 in there. So I come to see you and I say: Seaward, sorry, Seaward, Mr

23

Thornycroft…u…I think you made a mistake. I'm
expecting 260 quid and I only got 120 in here. And you
said to me: Uhu, that's your bonus. And I say: okay, so
where's my wages? And you say…I thought you said it
in a kind of funny…you know, having a joke kind of
way…you say: do you think you really deserve it? And I
say: Ha, ha! Yeh, well, you know, getting up at two in the
morning I think I deserve it, yes. So you say: okay, give
me the bonus back. So I give it back, thinking: the guy's
going to sort it out and I'm going to end up with my
260. TRUST! Only now I'm looking at my money and
all I got is 140 quid! 140 quid wages and no bonus!
(*Short pause.*) What you mean, yeh? So where's my
bonus? (*Pause.*) You're taking my bonus off me because I
damaged the van? But it was a wreck! That van nearly
killed me! I know what this is…while everyone here
is…while everyone here is just pissed off with the low
wages…take the Pole….the Pole, you know what he does
when he finishes here? He goes to paint toilets! The Pole
paints toilets in silence because he won't say anything to
you about his wages! I'm the only one who says it OUT
– who comes out with it…that's why you threaten my
life…The trouble with you Seaward – SEAWARD!
Okay. Your Dad invented this business here, yeh? This
fish mongery…and he hires us…your Dad – he's a SEA
man – he names you Seaward! He was looking at the sea
when he fucked your mother, maybe…You've never done
a day's work. Yeh, you come in here in the morning, stay
the day but if you don't you'd still get paid! You
probably hate me because you know when I come in
here I been out screwing all night. Maybe I have been.
Maybe it's just the smell of yesterday's fish! Or maybe
it's just what you think! But my bonus… I've got no
rights! You know? I'm your lackey and I've got no
rights…well… THAT's because we are in this city: this
city of lackeys. That is well known throughout the
Western World, this city of Cardiff, this City of Cardiff is
a city of lackeys: a city of Brain's drinkers and joke

tellers. You go into any pub and they all think they're great – they all think they know everything, all so fucking wise they don't want socialism, they don't want liberty, they don't want RIGHTS – they just want their SA and want to be able to tell you a joke because this city is a joke! Because it's run by people like you. Basically fucking English people like you! You don't even sell real fish! Well you sell fish that once swam but it's English! Grimsby! Your fish didn't even swim in Welsh waters! I'm leaving this city! This city of inadequates and slaves. This city of mediocrities and I'm going out West and I'm going to fish for real fish – Welsh fish and idealism! Fuck your job and your fucking bonus!

Lights down.

Scene 2

CARLO'S home. Friday morning.

CARLO comes on. He has greasy, swept-back black hair and a black moustache. He wears a red bandana and a soldier's tunic. He is carrying a mug of tea. He comes to the front of the stage looking out at the audience as though he's looking for someone. He is preoccupied. A little sad.

CARLO: Country. *Ducit amor patriae. (Pause.)* He's out there. He will come.
  (SERENA comes on with a mug of tea. She is a young woman of mixed race. CARLO turns to her.)
  Did you sleep well?
SERENA: Like a baby. Thanks. I feel...at home.
  (She sits at table occasionally drinking from the mug. CARLO turns to look out front again.)
  You know when you came into the pub last night...?
CARLO: I was looking for you.
SERENA: What do you mean?

25

CARLO: I was told that there was a beautiful young woman with the air of a Spaniard working there.

SERENA: (*Laughing.*) Yeh, yeh!

CARLO: (*Turning to look at her.*) There's a tone in your skin.

SERENA: My mother was black. From Guyana.

(*Silence. CARLO looks to front again.*)

Do you know Cardiff? The Docks?

CARLO: I've passed through.

SERENA: I needed to get out of the city. Especially that one. It just seems that between Friday and Friday there's this...emptiness. I'm on a Summer adventure!

(*CARLO goes to record player and puts music on. It's Act Two of Puccini's 'Tosca'.*)

(*Having to raise her voice a little above the music.*) What's this?

CARLO: Puccini. Tosca.

(*He turns music down a little.*)

Scarpia, the chief of police, is torturing the revolutionary Mario. Tosca's lover.

(*Pause.*)

SERENA: Thank you for letting me stay.

(*CARLO sits at table.*)

CARLO: It's a big house.

SERENA: It's huge! Beautiful. More like a mansion!

CARLO: Not so big.

SERENA: You should have been brought up in Maria Street like me. This is heaven!

(*Pause.*)

CARLO: Did you see the horse?

SERENA: Yes. It's beautiful. It's an appaloosa.

CARLO: You know?

SERENA: Yes. When I was a kid. Horses were my world. Appaloosas are American. The Spanish Conquistadors took them out there to the American West. The Indians called them magic dogs.

CARLO: The ancestors of my horse filled the plains with thunder and when the Indians finally got to master them they created such a ballet of outrage and beautiful violence!

SERENA: I like that!

CARLO: The parentage of the appaloosa can be traced back to times which inspired histories. To incidents which bore the burden of tragedy. To the beautiful, sweet-teared outcome of comedies.

SERENA: You should write a book on horses!

CARLO: Her history, her parentage is as rich as Shakespeare. Full with meaning. Compare that to us. Our history. The history of our people: you take a walk down a dirt path and come to a ravine.

SERENA: What people?

CARLO: Our people.

(*Silence. He gets up, picks up a book from a side-table and drops it on the table before her.*)

A history of Wales. Read it. You'll see that two great Roman historians – Tacitus and Dion Cassius argued over the parentage of the great Welsh Prince Caradog. The Romans felt that Wales was important enough to worry over the parentage of one of its princes. Was Caradog just a Silurian chief or the King of Britain? I worried over this, too, and was jailed.

SERENA: You were jailed?

CARLO: Yes.

SERENA: For doing what?

CARLO: For trying to discover the true parentage of the Welsh.

SERENA: That's really terrible. You shouldn't've bothered. Nobody much cares about it in Cardiff.

CARLO: I was jailed by my own people for fighting to liberate them.

SERENA: (*Looking out at audience.*) You must be famous. A hero!

CARLO: At the time all I could think about was my horses. (*Pause.*) When Caradog was finally conquered by the Romans after many great battles, he was taken to Rome. I imagined him, in procession to the centre of Rome, riding an appaloosa. That's what kept me going. He won the hearts of the Romans with a speech. With words!

SERENA: (*Turning back to CARLO.*) I should think you
could do that!
(*He smiles.*)

CARLO: It wasn't simply a question of *ave Caesar, morituri
te salutant,* this was the earning of respect. They saluted
him.

SERENA: When do you think the foal will come?

CARLO: When it's ready. We have to be patient. Strong.

SERENA: I'd say you have to belong.

CARLO: To what?

SERENA: To whatever. Family. You know. That's what
makes you strong.

CARLO: I had a strong father. He was leader of Spain.

SERENA: Your father was the leader of Spain?

CARLO: General Fransisco Franco! El Caudillo. (*Pause.*)
This tunic was his. He wore it throughout the Civil War.

SERENA: What Civil War?

CARLO: The Spanish Civil War. It was a time of great
suffering.

SERENA: Can I touch it?

CARLO: You mean, feel the history?
(*SERENA comes close to him and feels the tunic. They pause.
Silence.*)

SERENA: So you've got mixed blood. Like me.

CARLO: My mother died in Spain. I had all her dresses
sent over from there. They're upstairs.
(*CARLO touches SERENA's face.*)
Find one. We'll dance a tango.

SERENA: (*Laughing.*) But I can't dance the tango!

CARLO: I'll teach you. It's Friday. By Monday you'll dance
the tango.

SERENA: I've got to go back to the hotel.

CARLO: Why?

SERENA: My job!
(*Pause.*)

CARLO: And after that job?

SERENA: What?

CARLO: What will you do? Will you have anywhere to go?

SERENA: Not really.

CARLO: Go back to Cardiff and you'll live a miserable life of bitter failure. Looking for pleasure, finding boredom!
(*SERENA laughs.*)

SERENA: You've got it!

CARLO: Stay here! Look after my appaloosa. The foal can be yours.

SERENA: Don't you have a woman somewhere?

CARLO: A hero needs a heroine! I haven't found anyone suitable!
(*They laugh. He holds her tentatively.*)
Just stay! I could offer you a life of peace, of wisdom. A life of culture and heroism. And horses!

SERENA: You're serious!

CARLO: Just stay for a week! Try it! There's so much you can do. And I have so many things to show you.
(*SERENA looks around her with wonder.*)

SERENA: I can see. There's so much that's beautiful here.
(*Pause.*)

CARLO: You're wondering whether it'll be safe.

SERENA: Is it safe?

CARLO: It's safe.
(*Pause.*)

SERENA: I've got a few things that I'll have to get. From the hotel.
(*He goes to kiss her. She turns away as SION comes on.*)
There's someone here.
(*CARLO turns to SION.*)

CARLO: Where have you been?

SION: At the dole office.

CARLO: Last night?
(*CARLO turns the music off.*)

SION: I was depressed. They're trying to break me! I've got something wrong with my arse. I told the woman and she said: I don't think that should concern us here. She did not want to know! English bitch! I'm all clogged up! It's the stress!
(*CARLO takes SION a little to one side.*)

CARLO: (*Sotto voce with urgency.*) What is it this...this arse talk? You can't extemporise on your arse in front of a young woman with such contemporary abandon! Jesus Christ! What is it? Some oblique subterfuge?

SION: What...sorry, Carlo, she IS beautiful. I'm sorry, I can't...

CARLO: Sorry, no! Arse talk is disrespectful.

SION: I can't...I can't speak...I feel uncertain...

CARLO: Not SO uncertain!

SION: Well...I'm just trying to explain...I'm trying to explain why I haven't been here...you know...why...

CARLO: Okay. So let's end this arse essay – this colonal foray and get to the bottom of things...

SION: It's not...I was...this is just what I was saying to the woman in the dole office. They're all English down there, Carlo! It's a fucking conspiracy! They're contracted. Like hit men! They want us to...they get you down there and they want to...well they try to get you to fucking work! Doing what they want! So this is why I said I had arse trouble!

CARLO: Arse...you're using the word because it's...it's more aggressive? Your actual problem is with your bowels. Say bowels and the English will sense a logic; say arse and they will react with hostility.

SION: OK, Carlo! I'm sorry. Can we drop the arse thing? I didn't want to say it...I didn't mean to say it in front of her but sometimes...it's just one of those things...you know, sometimes someone is so beautiful the only way you can deal with the feeling of being...well...conquered is by saying something ugly. Because you feel so...so shy.

CARLO: Spoken like a true Welshman. Servile. How I hate the common herd: *Odi profanum vulgus et arceo.* Shy? No. Resentful – eaten up by resentment at being small enclosed...not shyness Sion, *resentiment* and it comes out in the darkest, most dismal way. Shy only in that you've been shy in coming round.

(*CARLO returns to SERENA to include her.*)

So where have you been? Have you forgotten about the project? You know how serious it is? You understand what it means for the country?

SION: I do!

CARLO: So where's your commitment?

SION: I was trying to say! Maybe if I finish…if I finish you'll see…

CARLO: No more talk of rectums?

SION: No, no!

CARLO: No, because she will go.

SION: She needn't go! Where will she go?

CARLO: (*To SERENA.*) Where will you go?

SERENA: Can I look for a dress?

CARLO: Yes! Upstairs. Go right to the end of the hall. The room on the left.

(*SERENA leaves happily.*)

SION: It was a lovely day, Carlo. I could have been hobbling. On the project. Aye, on the project. I said to this woman: do I have to be here? Is there a choice? She said: No. No choice. No fucking choice! An English bitch telling me I've got no choice in my own country! On the first day she stood there with her hand out welcoming everyone. This hippy came along and he wouldn't shake hands with her. He's English too so he can do it! He can deny her! That's what it's come to: a fucking hippy's got more rights in Wales than a Welshman. They had me in last Friday. Three hours. I got so frustrated I went home and smashed the washing machine. With a sledge. I've got four different sledge hammers and I took this one – it's a beauty and I flattened the machine. Then I took out of the middle this drum. It's beautiful. Looks like an Indian vase or something.

CARLO: But did you shake her hand?

SION: I had to!

(*CARLO makes a noise of disgust.*)

CARLO: When Caradog conquered Rome it was with a mere speech. But, it's said, one of the greatest speeches in recorded history. In the moment that he won the hearts of the people he became, as a Welshman, The King of Rome. I shoulder his mantle.

SION: What did he say?

CARLO: What?

SION: In his speech.

(*Pause.*)

CARLO: Find out. That's your homework.

SION: Don't joke, Carlo! Fucking hell! Anyway, I won't have time. I've got a job. In Newquay.

CARLO: Newquay?

SION: Yeh. They got me a job. Fixing fishing nets. Didn't you find anyone last night? A boy for the project?

CARLO: No.

SION: But you were so sure!

CARLO: Well I didn't! Your country will not forgive you if you let her down. Listen, what did you think of the girl?

SION: To be honest, Carlo, she looks like a wog!

CARLO: Where's your inner eye, man? The one that searches out what's possible not just what's seen? That same eye, in fact, that leads us on with our project to know that there is a nation here beyond the disorder of mediocrity. A nation of ideals; of vision. Imagine her in my mother's dress and you can imagine a country of academies where we teach in a language so rare in its teaching that we are gold and the envy of the world. Anyway, every man must have his piece of black arse. Part of growing up. You'll have yours some time. Only not this one.

SION: Why is she here?

CARLO: I've invited her to stay. Her presence will help with the appaloosa. Check the horse for me. Her success with her foal will be a metaphor for us. You know what a metaphor is?

SION: (*With a little laugh.*) Do I look like a hambone?
(*CARLO leaves with an almost military bearing.
SION follows, almost imitating him.*)

Lights down.

Scene 3

Newquay Harbour, West Wales. Saturday morning.

SION and BEN are sitting mending fish nets. In conversation, BEN is uncertain; tentative.

SION: (*Gruffly.*) I went to Cardiff once. It took a day to get there and you stay in castles for the night. That's how I remember it. And in the streets were black men and sometimes men in turbans and a lot of men like women. Homos I spose. And I thought: I'm too rough for Cardiff. Too violent. Too big a boy for those Irish streets.

BEN: I thought...I thought they were Welsh.

SION: What made you think that?

BEN: Well...they're in Cardiff. The capital.

SION: No Welshman would have laid the roads of the capital there in that place so easy for the English to get at. The Welsh would have built Cardiff on Cardigan Bay. My mother's mother married a mick so I know how the red-heads left the bogs of Ballybunion and found their natural way to that sink on the Bristol Channel that you call home.

BEN: Not me. I've disowned it. I was...um... too big for it too. So you're part Irish?

SION: Christ, no! My mother's mother had my mother conceived, born and wrapped in Welsh linen while the mick was still in Limerick. No. I'm Welsh through and through. But I'm interested in your too-big-for-Cardiffness. Has this ever burst out of you in any metaphor?

BEN: What d'you mean?

SION: Did you leave blood on any pavement or even pull the beard of some false Welshman posing with a pint of Brains when he knows that his ancestors are filth and rutted in the muds of Somerset? No, shit! I'm looking at you. You're a fucking nonentity. Why're you in West Wales?

BEN: I'm on the run.

SION: From what?

BEN: The police.

SION: Shoplifting eh? Or was it shirtlifting? Ha!

BEN: Something more terrible. (*Short pause.*) So you don't think I'm Welsh?

SION: I dunno. Siarad Cymraeg?

BEN: Tippin bach.

SION: Where'd you learn that? Changing buses in Llanllan? What's in your blood man? That's the fucking point.

BEN: Iron.

SION: Iron. Well that's hopeful. And when you spill it, what colour is it?

BEN: Red.

SION: Not green, then.

BEN: Why green?

SION: The colour of Wales.

BEN: I thought green was the colour of Ireland.

SION: They identify with our Celticness. Green is the colour of Plaid Cymru.

BEN: But the colour of, say, rugby is red. Welsh rugby.

SION: Aye, and there's red on the English flag. Red, white and blue!

BEN: Yeh! That red represents Wales! It's the Union Jack. There's no green on it.

SION: No! Because to the English, Wales doesn't exist!

BEN: But I think it's because green is Irish and Ireland is not part of Britain! Red is Wales. White is England and blue is Scotland!

SION: What are you? Some kind of English arse licker? You watch out for me, boy! I wiped the floor with a town-full of Lovells one Saturday night not six months ago!

BEN: But it would mean that the English have white blood!

SION: (*Thoughtful.*) White blood?

BEN: Like a lily.

SION: I like that. So if Welsh blood was red it would mean that the red in the blood of every man would be a recognition of the original Welshness of everyone.

BEN: Everyone except the English!

SION: (*Thoughtfully.*) In the veins of everyone who lives or has ever lived is the liquid of Welshness: on every blood-stained white shirt is the mark of Welshness; in the period of every woman is a flood of Welshness; in the slit wrists of every suicide is the evacuation of Welshness from a body too inadequate to contain it. This is marvellous! It's a lovely mountain-top madness. Wait till I tell Carlo!

BEN: Who's Carlo?

SION: Carlo? Carlo is a philosopher. Carlo is a soldier. Carlo is a lover. Carlo is a hunter. Carlo's tears make Llyn Brianne. Carlo steals into the bedrooms of Welsh innocence to dismember the English who fuck the Welsh there. Carlo is the dawn on Poppit Sands; the rough seas' calmer who whistles out the boats on beating eddies.

BEN: O, right.

SION: A man with no hint of mediocrity; a man of war, of violence and unselfish ambition. Nothing you could have done would be terrible enough to impress him. A man of rebellion and radicalism; inheritor of the great defiant spirit of Caradog of the Silurians who once conquered Rome with a speech. He taught me how to speak. He's a great teacher.

BEN: (*After a pause.*) Is this the same Carlo who went to jail for…

SION: For his country. Yes.

BEN: He must be a man of idealism.

SION: Idealism? He doesn't open his eyes without having a vision! And I'll tell you another thing: you wouldn't find him on the run! Not from anything.

(*Pause.*)

BEN: Would depend.

SION: On what?

BEN: On what he'd done.

SION: Like what?!

BEN: Like what I did. (*Pause.*) I killed a man.

SION: Huh! If you killed a man, I fuck horses!

BEN: I could give you the details.

SION: O *I* could give details – made up now: the murder of a man, head lopped off with a machete, body found in some fallow, unharrowed field. So easy to forge the details of a killing.

BEN: Yes but…I killed him with a fish.

SION: Poisoned him?

BEN: No. I brained him with a frozen salmon. At three in the morning on a cold, wet, fish-wholesaler's winter yard, Seaward Thornycroft died. It was easy to say that he slipped and knocked his head. We were the only two there and the fish itself was unscarred.

(Pause.)

SION: Tell me: give me one piece of information so fucking evilly original that will prove to me you're not lying because I would love to go to Carlo with this and bring him a bad godless fucker.

BEN: Is he a man who would recognise the gut anger and loneliness of one who feels abandoned, evicted within his own country?

SION: All other men have barely an inkling by comparison. Come on! Convince me!

(Pause.)

BEN: I could say that it's not possible to swing an icy salmon with bare hands, that you need felt gloves which are not worn in the loading – which implies premeditation; and I could say that the best place to hit is on the temple. I could say that you need to choreograph the hit so that you spin and catch him on the turn as he turns towards you. I could say that a fin of the fish broke off and pierced Seaward's eye…

(Pause.)

SION: Aye! Well? Are you going to say it?

BEN: Well.

SION: You mean you couldn't give a fuck if I believed you or not. Is that it?

BEN: Ye…yeh!

SION: So say it!

BEN: I couldn't give a fuck!

SION: Let me look into your eyes. That'll tell.

BEN: If you're a man of perception, that will tell.

(*SION comes close to BEN and looks deep into one eye.*)

SION: The eye of Ahab! (*Throws his arms around BEN.*) No man would leave the wasteland of Cardiff and come here to the heart of myth and antagonism with a story of how he laid out a man with a fish that was a lie. Knowing he would have more chance of rupturing the sky and reaching the stars than he would of escaping, if he was found out.

BEN: O, I've been to Sirius, Al Rischa, Pollux and Castor. (*Silence.*)

In my telescope.

SION: Ha, ha! (*SION hugs BEN.*)

Lights down.

Scene 4

CARLO's home. Saturday.

CARLO is teaching SERENA the tango. There is appropriate music. SERENA is wearing a beautiful dress. He swoops her down and pauses with her cradled in his arm.

CARLO: (*Mock dramatically.*) I am Carlo Fransisco Franco Lloyd Hughes.

SERENA: Named after him. D'you think I'm getting the hang of this?

CARLO: O yes. (*Pause.*) I'm going to call you Jeanne.

SERENA: Jeanne?

CARLO: After Jeanne Duval, Baudelaire's young Creole woman. A sometimes actress and sometimes whore. A woman of devastating arms and legs.

SERENA: I don't think I like that!!

CARLO: Don't get angry! He was obsessed with her. (*Pause.*)

SERENA: Thanks for last night.

CARLO: For what?

SERENA: For not trying to get me into your bed. Again. It's much more romantic.

CARLO: Your romanticism! (*Dramatically.*) I was born in Babylon of a Spanish whore whose ancestors were merchants who owned vast tracts of the Orient! That's what you want to believe. I belong to that pantheon of leaders who can make nations of a foreign Prince's mortmain.

SERENA: That's not what I meant! I thought...most people I know live from Friday to Friday get some sex then get married. This was different.

CARLO: Will you want me tonight? It can't be because of some whimsical interpretation of me.

SERENA: How can I interpret you? I hardly know you!

CARLO: We must keep it real. Like the project which must never succumb to merely satisfying the craving for the romantic at the expense of doing battle for the real! Watch the romanticism. You'll give fascism a bad name!

SERENA: (*After a pause.*) Fascism? Why fascism? Anyway I thought fascism HAD a bad name.

(*CARLO suddenly stops.*

SERENA is caught in a pose in which she is falling back over his knee and he is supporting her. He lowers his head over her.)

CARLO: (*With mock romanticism.*) So you don't want to be my lover?

SERENA: I was just wondering why you were talking about fascism!!

(*Silence.*

CARLO suddenly laughs loudly.)

CARLO: Marvellous! You're shocked by the word. Don't be. We make of words what we need to make of them.

(*He throws his other arm around her embracing her and kissing her.*

She laughs.)

SERENA: My appaloosa!

(*SION bursts on.*)

CARLO: Christ, man! D'you have no decorum? Can't you knock?

SION: I've found him!
> (*CARLO lifts SERENA up.*
> *SION looks at her wide-eyed.*)

CARLO: Who?

SION: The boy for the project! Carlo, this boy...this boy...he's...forget your Charlie Mansons, Burke and Hare, Son of Sam, Dutch Schultz – all of them...I'll set the scene...
> (*SION turns off the record player.*)

CARLO: Make this quick!

SION: I'll tell it to you as he told it to me! Word for word! Picture: three o'clock – a cold winter's morning in the city of pomegranates...

CARLO: Pomegranates? What?...
> (*SERENA laughs.*)

SION: Cardiff! Can I speak in front of her?

CARLO: Yes, yes!
> (*CARLO stands SERENA up and unhandles her.*)

SION: A fish wholesaler's yard. The boss is a giant of a man called Seaward: an ex-sailor who, it's said, ripped the throat out of a Petty Officer for interrupting his ablutions and hung his oesophagus over the port rail. This man ran the yard and all the drivers were afraid of him. He used to run a protection racket: if someone didn't pay he'd have his truck sabotaged by Seaward only he wouldn't know what it was going to be: brakes, tyres, you know. On top of all this, Seaward was English. On the morning in question, our boy – Ben – tired from a night of sexual excess and in no mood for the insults and threats, at the first sight of a snide remark and to the greater glory of Wales, picked up a three foot frozen salmon and walloped the great Sais Seaward with it, decapitating the bugger. The other men then, in awe now of our Ben, rigged up an elaborate structure of scaffolding and some ice like a blade to make it look like an accident.

SERENA: (*Scoffingly.*) A fish!?

CARLO: And you've seen this boy?

SION: I was working with him!

CARLO: (*More than a little interested.*) What does he look like?

SION: That's the beauty of it! Looks nothing at all like a killer. Doesn't even look hard!

CARLO: Then how do you know? How can you be sure?

SION: See a man with a broken nose flat against his face – the picture of terror. But that's not a hard man. The hard man's the one who did it. The hard man has a refined, unbroken nose. BUT – calloused knuckles...

CARLO: And he...?

SION: ...has spent a lifetime punching bone.

SERENA: Why get so excited about a fishmonger?

CARLO: Wales needs this boy! He is the one I've been waiting for! And now I feel a curious...almost sexual excitement! Great surges of manhood rising in me! I see my brain in a jar with formaldehyde in a case in the National Museum of Wales, idolised by generations of Welsh to come. I feel unmitigated self-appreciation and the warmth of self love! It's you, Serena! You've come to me and brought refinement to my politics.

SERENA: What refinement?

CARLO: My word...fascism. It bothers you because you think it might be racist.

SERENA: I should think so!

CARLO: But my fascism is the fascism of Rome!

SERENA: So you're a fascist?

CARLO: But not a racist!

SERENA: I don't understand that.

CARLO: The racist is the liberal bourgeois. Our police are racist, our judges are racist, our teachers are racist. I'm breaking away from them all! From them AND their racism! When my father, Franco, invaded Spain to liberate it, he did so at the head of black troops from Africa! Fascism is strong. Racism is weak! You've made me see this! You have brought luck to my endeavours! (*To SION.*) Get him here! As soon as possible! This evening! Now!

SION: But I won't see him until tomorrow!

CARLO: Find him! He is in West Wales! He's not on the fucking moon!

SION: Okay. (*SION goes to leave.*)

CARLO: No! Wait! Serena, please, go quickly and check the appaloosa.

(*SERENA leaves looking perplexed.*)

I saw the way you looked at her.

SION: It was nothing Carlo! I...I....

CARLO: Christ, Sion! I don't see you as a rival! I'm talking about that recognition. I'm overwhelmed by her! I think I could marry her! It's all come together now: the appaloosa, her and now this boy for the project!

SION: He is the boy for the project!

CARLO: It's like...

SION: It's like a soup of metaphors!

(*Pause.*)

CARLO: A soup! Go and find him!

(*SION leaves.*)

Lights down.

Scene 5

The same, later.

CARLO is sitting at the table facing the audience. At the centre of the table there is a bottle of whisky. There are four glasses and three other chairs – two chairs, one with CARLO in, facing the audience, the others at each end of the table. SERENA is sitting at left end of table. She still wears the dress.

SERENA: I'm going to name the foal Ruby after my mother. It was she who told me about coming here to the West. She always said: The West owes me.

CARLO: The West owes her?

SERENA: Yes. I don't know what she meant. Something happened sometime. I never asked her because I felt it must have been terrible. (*Pause.*) If it's a colt I'll call it Dennis.

CARLO: Dennis? Benito!

SERENA: Benito?

CARLO: After the great romantic fascist and freedom fighter Mussolini!

SERENA: My horse won't be a fascist! I was brought up to believe that all fascists are bastards.

CARLO: Garibaldi, Mussolini, Nasser made their countries! They were fascist! Even David Ben-Gurion who made Israel was! But because he was a Jew and the Jews were killed by fascists people will say he wasn't. But he was to the dead British soldiers! And I will say he was a fascist because he made a country! And to make a country here in Wales I will say: I am a fascist!

SERENA: But why do you want to use that word?

CARLO: It is only a word!

SERENA: It's a bit more than that!

CARLO: Not exactly! We must struggle like the Palestinians or the Irish because we're not just people living in a place called Wales, we are A People! Not a whole conglomerate of different kinds of people who were never Welsh – mostly English – who are now in Wales. Your mother was a Negress. A Welsh Negress. Does it make sense to say that?

SERENA: Why not?

CARLO: O I want to say it! I want to say she's Welsh. To say with one determined voice: we are here, all of us, Welsh. But how do we do it? I say: through Fascism! There's no other way to do it. My father Franco, he made a country. You won't make a country as a liberal bourgeois. This is what we need the men in the pubs of the nation's capital to speak of!

SERENA: More likely they'd be talking about women or ferrets.

CARLO: But any mention of Wales and fascism – our strength and I suppose they'd scoff! Don't you worry about the word. Worry about that!

SERENA: But do we have to talk about this all the time? Or can't you call it something else? Isn't there a Welsh word?

CARLO: (*He bangs table, impatient and a little angry.*) I'll make one up! Here and now!

SERENA: Why're you getting so angry? It's up to you. (*Pause.*)

CARLO: Priciaeth!

SERENA: Priciaeth?!

CARLO: Aye! Pric means stick and the facses were a bunch of sticks so Priciaeth! That would make me a pricydd. (*SERENA laughs.*)

SERENA: Well that definitely doesn't sound so terrible! (*Pause.*) When the foal comes we can go out riding together. Like landed gentry!
(*She laughs.*
SION and BEN come on.
BEN and SERENA immediately focus on one another.
CARLO eyes BEN with wonder.)

SION: This is Ben.
(*CARLO gets up and immediately embraces BEN heartily.*)

CARLO: Ben! Sit ye down!
(*BEN sits at end of the table opposite SERENA.*
SION sits beside CARLO. They all look at each other in silence for a moment. Smiles etc.)
(*To BEN.*) Have a drink!
(*CARLO pushes the bottle vigorously to BEN.*
BEN takes bottle and pours himself a drink.)

SERENA: So you're from Cardiff. What part?

BEN: (*After a pause.*) All of it.
(*BEN slides bottle across table to SERENA.*)

CARLO: All of it! Ha! Yes! That's good!

SION: Because he's disowned it. If he was from only a part he could only disown a part!
(*SERENA pours drink.*)

CARLO: And have you abandoned the city because of…um…a certain event or because…well…because?…
(*SERENA slides bottle across to CARLO.*)

BEN: Because it's a city with nothing. No identity. Its people trade in second hand jokes.

CARLO: Maybe the *culte de la blague*? – The cult, or you may say, culture of the joke, which began with

Baudelaire, has become fundamental to fascist
propaganda.

SERENA: Is it because Cardiff is a fascist city that you left
it?

BEN: If it was then it'd be a fascist city by accident. Even
fascism has, I don't know, something like ideals I
suppose.

SERENA: What ideals?

CARLO: The *culte de la blague!* Joke as act of cruelty.
Cardiff has the jokes but not the cruelty.

BEN: Yes! It needs to become a place of…of killing for
justice! Killing for idealism.

SERENA: Murder!

BEN: Well…if that's what it is, yeh. Okay.

SERENA: Murder's the opposite of justice!

SION: Well what about what Ben himself did? He had no
choice.

BEN: I was cheated…

SION: There was no other way of dealing with the monster
Thornycroft.

CARLO: Murder in pursuit of idealism!
     (*SION takes bottle from CARLO.*)

SERENA: I've heard of murder in pursuit of cocaine. What
you're talking about would be something else.

CARLO: Like what?
     (*CARLO takes bottle back and pours.*)

BEN: An act of retribution? Or vengeance?

CARLO: But what's wrong with murder? Why not call a
spade a spade? Shilly-shallying has no place in idealism.
And whether you like it or not, Serena, you can't say that
there's no link between murder and justice. Capital
punishment is murder! Camus called it administrative
murder! What is the taking of a life by another under
any circumstance if not murder? No philosopher would
argue with that!
     (*CARLO slides bottle to SERENA.*)

SERENA: Something like Priciaeth.

BEN: What's that?

CARLO: Welsh extremism!

BEN: Never heard of it.

CARLO: It's new!

BEN: Maybe it's something like this: a jury makes the decision in a murder case. But, if the most perfect murder is premeditated then nothing could be more premeditated than twelve people deliberating on the fate of an individual knowing that the decision could end with his death as happens in more advanced democracies like America.

CARLO: Brilliant! Ha, ha! (*To BEN.*) Tell us about yours.

BEN: Mine?

(*SERENA slides bottle to BEN.*)

SERENA: The fish!

CARLO: Aye! The mighty fish!

BEN: Well…um…it was…I was driven to it. (*Pours.*) Over a lifetime, really. I was getting more and more angry. Frustrated with the city. It's emptiness of any ideal. I used to think: I'd love to see the beer drinkers choke on their fear as though they had seen a scorpion in their last mouthful. I would love to see the garrulous have their teeth pulled in mid word and the joke tellers have their tongues burnt in the punch line. The city is terrorised by smugness: that smugness which is the defence of inadequacy.

CARLO: You have a way with words. I like that!

BEN: As a young man, with my friends, instead of taking a short cut through one of Cardiff's shopping arcades on our Saturday afternoon cruising, we'd take the street route because there would be more skirt to clock. This was the summit of our ambition! This was the journey to idealism the city had inspired in us! And at night, what else could we do but make love to the young women in the narrow streets, on street corners, in the backs of buses, in the public toilets sometimes three, maybe four a night and then, in the despair that comes with satiation, drown ourselves in the bitter liquid of…well…bitter.

SERENA: But what about the fish?

BEN: All this led up to the fish!

SERENA: How big was it?

BEN: Well...about...about...

SION: About three foot you told me.

(BEN slides bottle to SION.)

BEN: Yes. Maybe longer.

(BEN shows a measure with his hand.)

CARLO: A noble creature, then. Fit for the job.

BEN: Yes!

CARLO: And you picked it up....

(CARLO gets up and mimes what he describes.)

BEN: By the tail.

SERENA: It must have been difficult to get a grip.

BEN: I had some special felt gloves, stashed, ready...

CARLO: Premeditation!

BEN: Yes.

CARLO: In pursuit of justice.

SERENA: *(Ironically.)* And idealism.

CARLO: Aye!

(CARLO takes bottle from SION then resumes his pose with imaginary fish.)

And so you....

(CARLO suddenly stops.)

Sion! We have such a fish!

SION: What?

CARLO: In the freezer! From Dai Dynamite. Christ, must be six months ago.

(CARLO gets up and leaves.)

SERENA: *(To BEN, a little hostile.)* I know Thornycrofts. I've passed there. It always seemed so peaceful. *(Pause.)* I feel as if I know you.

BEN: I think I've got one of those faces. Maybe you've seen me in Newquay.

SERENA: No. Cardiff. D'you go to the Philharmonic?

BEN: Yeh. I've been there. Do you know Sammy Erskine?

SERENA: What, the black kid who does the dope?

BEN: Yeh.

SERENA: No, I don't know him. I see him round. Do you do dope?

BEN: I've smoked a few joints.

SERENA: Have you got any with you?

SION: What are you on about?

SERENA: Dope. Marijuana. You ever tried it?

SION: No, I haven't. No.

SERENA: You haven't lived!

BEN: (*To SION.*) There's none here? In this neck of the woods?

SION: There's loads of it. Only I don't want to touch it.

SERENA: Why?

SION: It's not a Welsh thing to do.

SERENA: Go to Pontypridd!

(*BEN laughs.*)

SION: (*Angrily.*) The hippies in the hills grow the stuff in the forestry. We know that. English hippies growing foreign drugs in a Welsh forest is not a fucking metaphor. It's something we'll have to do something about.

(*Silence.*)

SERENA: (*To BEN.*) I really feel like I know you.

(*Pause.*)

SION: It'll be a laugh to redo the killing.

BEN: What do you mean?!

SION: To swing the fish a bit.

BEN: O.

SERENA: Perhaps it'll clear things up.

(*CARLO returns.*)

CARLO: I can't find the fucker! There's a fucking ox in there that needs shifting! Go and do it, Sion.

(*SION leaves.*

SERENA and BEN are looking at each other as CARLO pours a drink. He pauses and looks at the other two.)

So what about the sex? Are you a sexual man now?

(*CARLO slides bottle to BEN.*)

BEN: I'm....um...like any man. I suppose. A victim of it.

CARLO: Bravo! No people has ever suffered that victimhood like the Welsh. Even the Negro is conceded his enormous member, though it sticks in the throat of the Englishman.

SERENA: That's racist.

CARLO: It's what the racist English say. And for the English, the Welsh shag sheep. The Welsh are insensitive, ball-centric – by which I mean testes – Rugby players or the shaggers of sheep. My advice to you in the throes of your idealism, is to sublimate your sexuality. Adopt the posture of Nietzsche, the syphilitic philosopher condemned to death by his urges, and lift the energy of those urges to a plain where they may be of some use in the waging of war upon those who would so maliciously characterise your people. *Vae victis!* Woe to the vanquished!

BEN: I'll give it some thought.

CARLO: (*Hits table.*) No! Don't squander the moment you have in history on vanity! Because it is vanity. That power you experience in the moment you dominate and vanquish a woman will, in a celestial second be gone! You'll be frail, your muscles no more tense than a poppy stem; your eyes dull like a frosted window and your cock! – your cock will only be hard to piss through! While your people – your people are eternal!
(*Pause.*)

BEN: I'm not afraid to seize the moment for a greater consideration. To do what needs to be done.

CARLO: O, Christ, I know! *Carpe diem!* How many have addressed their oppression like you? Few! But that was for yourself. Now you must do it for your people.

BEN: That's what I want, yeh. But do you think I have to give up sex?
(*SION has returned and is standing slightly in the shadow holding a frozen salmon.*)

CARLO: I'm talking about the corralling of all your energies and, in the thought of doing that, being conscious of the sublime nature of the effort.

SERENA: Or better still, go back to Newquay and get yourself laid.

SION: But Carlo's only speaking like....well, like... metaphorically.

(*They turn to SION as he comes into the light with the fish.*)

CARLO: The fish!

(*CARLO gets up and takes the fish.*)

BEN: In other words I need not cut my balls off.

CARLO: (*Laughing.*) Christ no! Though I dare say you'd be the man to do it! Right!

(*CARLO comes before the table to give himself room. He has the fish by the tail and begins to lift it.*)

No, no! Gloves! Get my gauntlets, Sion! In the hallway. (*SION goes.*)

These are beauties! Franco's own. Given to my mother.

BEN: Franco?

CARLO: Aye.

BEN: What, you mean Spanish Franco?

CARLO: Aye, the very one. The Caudillo.

BEN: Wasn't Franco a vicious dictator?

(*Pause.*)

CARLO: Wasn't Churchill?

BEN: Was he?

CARLO: He slaughtered our miners!

SERENA: His gloves strangled Welshman without mercy.

CARLO: Spoken like a daughter of Caradog!

(*SION comes on with gloves.*)

There they are! (*He puts gauntlets on.*) Right, talk me through it. Sion, you'll have to be the big fish fucker himself. (*To BEN.*) He was six foot six?

(*The three are standing before the table.*)

BEN: (*Bemused.*) Six foot six?

CARLO: A monster, as Sion said.

BEN: O, yeh! Yes.

CARLO: We need to know where his neck would be. Give just over a foot for the head and we're talking just under five foot six which would be just about the top of Sion's

ear. Right. One more technicality. The head came off.
How was that?

BEN: The head? The fish head?

CARLO: No! The fucker's head!

(*Pause.*)

SERENA: Well the head did come off didn't it?

BEN: Yes! Yes. Clean off!

CARLO: Right. So how?

BEN: How?

CARLO: Yes! How did you cleave the fucker's head off?

BEN: Well...I just hit him.

CARLO: Yes, but how did you hold the fish? Was it the
dorsal? Did you hold it so that the dorsal became the
blade?

BEN: (*Affecting boldness.*) Of course! There's no other way!

CARLO: Aye! But it needs to be established.

(*CARLO holds fish with the dorsal upward so that as he
swings back, he can turn it to its side.*)

So where was he standing?

BEN: Well...let's say...

(*He goes to SION and positions him with his back to CARLO.*)

CARLO: And you snuck up behind him... (*Pause.*) Tell
me...what were you thinking?

BEN: I was thinking – I'm going to hit him.

CARLO: Of course you were thinking that! But how? How
were you feeling? What were you feeling?

BEN: I was...I was feeling angry!

CARLO: (*Suddenly angry himself.*) Not angry! Not just angry!
More!

BEN: Well no! Of course not! (*Exploding suddenly in mock
rage with his face contorted etc..*) I was thinking I'm going
to get you you ugly fucker! You're going to pay!

CARLO: Lovely! Right! (*He positions himself and begins to lift
the fish. He is obviously struggling.*) Ai, ai, ai! (*He steps back.*)
Need to practise my swing! (*He attempts to swing the fish
but can't.*) It can't be done.

BEN: It can.

CARLO: It can't be done!

BEN: I did it!

CARLO: Right! Do it again for me. Now!

(*Silence.*)

BEN: No!

CARLO: I'm telling you! Now!

SION: Can I turn around?

CARLO: No.

BEN: But...

SERENA: Maybe he can't do it now, Carlo, because he's not feeling the anger! It's the anger that gave him his strength.

CARLO: I'm not asking him to DO it. I just want to see the swing!

SERENA: But anger has to be at the root! If there's no anger nothing can be done!

BEN: She's right. And I swore, after the decapitation, that I would only ever again summon up that kind of anger if it's in a just cause. A cause in pursuit of a great ideal. Like, say, the liberating of one's nation.

CARLO: Bravo!

(*Suddenly, with a superhuman effort, CARLO swings the fish towards SION.*)

BEN/SERENA: Duck!

(*SION hits the floor as the fish just misses him.
CARLO overbalances and he, too, hits the floor. Silence.
CARLO clumsily gets to his feet, furious with SION.*)

CARLO: Why did you duck you twat? You're in the front line! (*Goes to SION and shouts at him.*) What kind of army do you think we're creating here? Tell me that you're more than just a constipated little runt! It's galling to have had such a spectacle in front of Ben – currently the boldest and most successful Welshman alive! Get up!

(*SION gets up. He looks resentful and angry but is silent.
CARLO goes to BEN and puts an arm around him.*)

Let's have a drink! Sion, take that fish back.

(*SION leaves with fish.
They sit at table.*)

So, there's not even a residue of idealism in our great
capital city.
(*Pause.*)

BEN: I had a landlord once called Cecil. Black guy. I used
to keep using this washer in the electric meter and when
he emptied it he'd always give me the washer back.
Hoping that one day I wouldn't use it. That was the only
trace of idealism I found anywhere.

CARLO: (*To SERENA.*) You see? A black man!

BEN: But even that was tarnished.

CARLO: In what way?

BEN: He was a homosexual. He wanted me in his bed.
I never knew if that was the real reason for giving the
washer back.

CARLO: Place is a cess pit!

BEN: No ideals and no democracy.

CARLO: Do you mean that English game in which the
people are confounded by the complexities of the rules
and the rules' clauses and sub-clauses? Democracy is an
English word.

BEN: I thought it was Greek.

CARLO: It's all Greek! Ha! The only way you can
convince the English of democratic values is by
bombing them. The Welsh don't need democracy. They
need strong leadership and a few hardy myths.
(*SION returns and sits at table.*
SERENA puts a hand on his arm. He looks at her with
hostility.
BEN sees this.
SERENA looks hurt.
CARLO pours drinks.)

BEN: Do you think that in this country, everyone should
have their own identity or the identity of their country?

SERENA: Does it matter? Why does any of this matter?
Why can't we talk about something else?

CARLO: (*After a pause.*) We should, all of us, have our
identity as individuals and our identity as belonging to
the country through the language. This is why the Welsh

language is important. If you can't speak your language
you don't have a culture!

BEN: But I can't speak Welsh.

CARLO: But you have a dispensation because of your
particular exceptional talent that may be used in the
service of the language! You see, Ben, the English have
made you give up your language in order to make you
English! But this language was the first language of
Britain. We must fight or eventually there'll be only one
language and that will be a kind of English. English is a
'fuck you!' language. Anyone who speaks English is
saying: 'Fuck you!' Put it this way: it's easier to say 'fuck
you' in English than it is in German.

SERENA: That's because 'fuck you' is English. On the
other hand the 'fuck you' might be English but the
intention could be Chinese.

CARLO: Chinese?

BEN: Yeh. A Chinese person speaking English might say
'fuck you' but he's saying it as a Chinese. A Chinaman.
Not as an Englishman. Don't you think so?

CARLO: Fuck you! Aye, fuck you. And also, fuck you for
the future. Because with the fuck yous there is no future.
The only thing you can be certain of is the past. If you
want any kind of status, any kind of presence on this
globe, you have to find it in the past. If you want
progress then I can tell you a time will come when there
won't be any Welsh living in Wales. What will Wales
mean then?

BEN: You said your mother knew Franco?

CARLO: Yes.

BEN: Was she Spanish?

CARLO: No. He was.

BEN: I know that but...

CARLO: (*To the other two.*) Shall I tell him?

SERENA: Franco was Carlo's father.

CARLO: Franco was my real father. My reputed father was
a professor of English and, to me, a great
disappointment. When is a professor of English ever

anything more than just a gnat on the back of a
Shakespeare or a Dickens or a Jane Austen? Especially
in this country! My reputed father taught all three. A
Welsh professor of English! And I'll tell you how he
ended his life: like a sore! To begin with. Then, later, a
stain. A stain on a sheet my mother brought back from
the Alcazar. Where she once enjoyed the sexual
attentions of the Caudillo, my father.
(*Silence.*)

BEN: Now I come to think of it, you look Spanish.

CARLO: What does that mean? To look Spanish. Many of
the Irish in Galway are Spanish!

BEN: O, no! I don't think it matters. It's good that you're
part Spanish. I'm just wondering about the English who
might be part Welsh.

CARLO: What English are those?

BEN: Well...a lot of the people of Birmingham are or were
Welsh.

CARLO: (*Suddenly angry.*) They chose to live in England! If
you speak with a Birmingham accent and vote for
English MPs, you're English! You can't be Welsh and
live in England. It makes no fucking sense!
(*He smashes his fist down on the table. Pause.*)

SERENA: So – can you be English and live in Wales?

SION: The English who live in Wales don't want to be
Welsh. They want to stay English! That's why they want
to get rid of the language of the Welsh! Make it all sound
English and it becomes England!

SERENA: (*To SION.*) What about those from the Caribbean
who came to Wales? They have their identity but don't
expect to turn Wales into Jamaica!

SION: That's...that's just a metaphor!
(*Pause.*)

CARLO: (*To BEN.*) Join us. We have a project. (*Pause.*) How
far would you be prepared to go to help us? Is there
anything you wouldn't do?

BEN: Well... No.

CARLO: And would you be prepared to use your special skills? Those exemplified in the episode of the fish? (*Pause.*)

BEN: You mean: would I, for example, assassinate the Secretary of State for Wales with, perhaps, an Atlantic cod? Yes!

(*Silence. All look surprised.*)

CARLO: Sion! Get the music!

SION: Which...?

CARLO: The band! The band!

(*SION goes to record player.*)

(*To SERENA about BEN.*) You know? I love this boy! I'm going to teach him everything I know! (*To BEN.*) I'm going to teach you everything I know!

BEN: Good. That'll be good.

CARLO: You can be my protégé.

BEN: It's all happened so quick!

SERENA: (*To CARLO.*) I'd be interested to know if he's got some talent besides killing people with fishes. (*Pause.*)

(*CARLO laughs.*

SION is standing by record player looking dismayed and even angry.)

CARLO: (*To SION impatiently.*) Have you found it?

SION: Aye!

CARLO: Well put it on then!

(*SION is about to put on record.*)

Wait! Before you do – Sion, I want you on the tuba. Ben, the drum...

BEN: What...I don't get...

CARLO: You'll see. Serena, cymbals and me: I'll lead. Music!

(*SION puts on music. It's German marshal music.*

All line up behind CARLO.)

BEN: Sounds like German – Nazi music.

CARLO: Sion. Stop it a minute.

(*SION stops music.*)

Nazi. What is Nazi? Only a word. Our liberal bourgeoisie would deprecate Puccini by saying that he was a fascist as though fascism is the enemy of Art. And yet, those same people, in their expensive seats and in their circles of enlightenment like nothing more than a good old-fashioned fascist opera whether it's Puccini or Wagner! And it doesn't end there! The sentiments of the culture that you see all around you have been delivered by notable fascists or those so far to the right it makes no difference: Baudelaire! Yeats! Eliot! Camus! And our own Saunders Lewis! Sion! Music!

(*All line up behind CARLO again as music begins.*
They march around the space miming with their imaginary
instruments. Lights go down as they march.)

PART TWO

Scene 1

The same. Later.

BEN is looking through records. He selects one and puts it on. It's Beethoven's Fifth Symphony. He conducts an imaginary orchestra. SERENA comes on. She coughs. BEN stops abruptly, embarrassed. He takes the record off. SION is eavesdropping on this scene.

SERENA: You shouldn't've stopped.

BEN: I was...um...just excercising.

SERENA: Why're you here?

BEN: I could tell you didn't like me straight away.

SERENA: It doesn't feel good to me.

BEN: Why not?

SERENA: I think you could bring out the worst in him. Do you do much exercise?

BEN: What? Like walking? Running?

SERENA: Pumping iron. That sort of thing.

BEN: A bit, yeh. I've done a bit. I've got dumb bells.

SERENA: You must have pretty good muscles.

BEN: Just your average, probably.

SERENA: But you swung the fish!

BEN: You don't need that big. It's technique.

SERENA: Your technique must be good.

BEN: I've had a lot of practice. In the dark hours of night with a turbot or a tuna from the Black Sea.
(*Pause.*)

SERENA: I know of people who get killed in The Bay – crack, heroin dealers but that's...that's different. I mean...don't you feel terrible? To have killed someone? Is it something that comes natural to you? Killing.

BEN: No. I felt terrible. It happened in a split second. It was just...you know...

SERENA: And to have done it with a fish!

BEN: Yeh.

SERENA: I'm surprised you're so calm.

BEN: How d'you know I'm calm? I could be raging inside.
(*Pause.*)

SERENA: Is it true what they say about skate?

BEN: What's that?

SERENA: I've heard that before the fishermen can land the
fish they have to cut out the...the genitals of the fish
because they look so much like a woman's.

BEN: I have heard that. But by the time we get the skate it's
just the wings packed in boxes.

SERENA: The wings of a skate. Sounds...nice. But what a
price to pay – cutting out its womanhood.
(*Pause.*)

BEN: Better that than have the fish drive men to acts of
sexual depravity.
(*Pause.*)

SERENA: Can I feel them? Your muscles?
(*BEN rolls his sleeve up tentatively.*
SERENA feels his arm. She's not too impressed.)
Why are you here?

BEN: They asked me over.

SERENA: They want you to help them with this project.

BEN: (*Dismissively.*) Whatever that is.

SERENA: Yes, but whatever it is will be serious!

BEN: I can handle it! I grew up on Cardiff's mean streets!

SERENA: O yeh, well – I just hope you know what you're
doing.

BEN: Hey! *I* killed a man with a fish!
(*Pause.*)

SERENA: (*Suddenly erupting.*) Maybe you think he's a
crackpot! Famous because he went to jail for his country.
Locked up by his own people! In Cardiff I can imagine
everyone thinking: what a twat! Maybe you think this is
just a great way to spend a night in the country! At the
home of a famous crackpot!

BEN: I don't think any of that!

SERENA: Well don't, because he's not a crackpot!

(*Pause.*)

SERENA: Let me tell you: what really worries me is that you're not taking this seriously!

BEN: Well maybe it's not so serious! How do you know? Do you think he really believes whatever it is he believes?

SERENA: O he believes it! But he believed in it as long as it never had to happen. Now you've turned up and he believes in you and believes that now it could happen! You're making him believe that this thing he didn't really believe could happen, can. Or let me put it another way: you're going to fuck up what I've got going here if you keep him focused on this fucking project!

BEN: But you're the one who told him I couldn't do it because I wasn't angry which means I could have done it if I was!

SERENA: That's because I was concerned about you getting into something there and then that you couldn't get out of. And building up his hopes only to have him disappointed if you could never do it! So why don't you just go!

(*Pause.*)

BEN: It would be impolite.

(*SERENA gasps and leaves.*)

Lights down.

Scene 2

The same. Later that evening.

CARLO, still wearing tunic, is sitting at table looking at audience, smoking a small cigar. Open on the table is a map of Wales – the project map. There is also a full bottle of whiskey and the gauntlets. There is music from Puccini playing. This will develop into a love aria. As soon as the singing begins, CARLO stands up and mimes to it. When it finishes, he turns record player off and sits.

CARLO: (*To audience.*) *Amor vincit omnia.* Love conquers all. She's gone up. I'll let her prepare before I present

myself. The lover: warm-blooded. Italian, fascist.
Spaniard, fascist. Argentinian! Fascist. Welsh: priccydd.
The non-lover. Cold blooded. Russian. Communist. The
Fascist brings with him the warmth of history and night,
the Communist, the coldness of tomorrow which is
always dead because you can never get there. And who
was the proto fascist par excellence? Casanova! The
lover doesn't just take off his clothes, he takes off his
skin and he digs into his chest and he rips out his heart
and he hands it to her and he says: take it, I can give you
no more and I can give you no less. In the act of love
the lover keeps nothing for himself. He becomes this
new thing. He has subsumed his existence within a
greater thing. It's an act of dying and as you finish the
last nail is put into the coffin. You negate yourself! Keats
called it negative capability! Art through love through
death. When I was younger I was told: if you want a
vigorous sex life, go in for extreme politics. I know
Marxists who knew less about dialectical materialism
than delectable copulation! The politician is always self-
obsessive while the lover must always be selfless and
giving. Which is what I will be like tonight with Serena.
(*CARLO takes a deep breath.*

SION comes on.)
What's the matter? Restless? (*Mischievously.*) Thinking
about me and my Serena?

SION: No.

CARLO: Come on! What do you think of her? Really.

SION: I told you.

CARLO: Come on Sion, you fucker!

SION: Okay. She's pretty.

CARLO: Pretty? Pretty fucking sultry! It's that bit of black
in her.

SION: Yeh.

CARLO: Have you ever had ANY piece of arse?

SION: Of course I have! Loads!

CARLO: Like who?

(*Pause.*)

SION: Delyth Jones.

CARLO: Christ! Delyth Jones is everyone's first! She's not much more than the sock you wank off into!

SION: (*Hurt.*) Well is this your first time with a black woman?

CARLO: No! God no. No, my first was twenty years ago.

Lights down.

Scene 3

Cardiff. Twenty years earlier.

CARLO comes on with RUBY. Both are a little drunk.

RUBY: Sit down.
   (*CARLO sits.*
   RUBY sits on his lap.)
   Have you done it before?

CARLO: What? IT?

RUBY: Yes.

CARLO: Jesus, yes! I'm from Cardiganshire. They do it to sheep down there!
   (*RUBY laughs.*)

RUBY: I haven't heard that before. But it sounds quite sad.

CARLO: No! Some of those hambones are lucky to get off with a bit of mutton!
   (*Pause.*
   RUBY holds CARLO's face.)

RUBY: I can help you.

CARLO: What d'you mean?

RUBY: You're...uncertain.

CARLO: I'm alright. Really!
   (*RUBY strokes his face.*)

RUBY: What's your name?

CARLO: Franco.

RUBY: That sounds...exotic. Romantic.

CARLO: You look exotic. Where are you from?

RUBY: Cardiff.

CARLO: No, I mean…

RUBY: What?

CARLO: Colour…you've got..

RUBY: I'm black. From Guyana. What used to be British Guyana. Is this your first time in the big city?

CARLO: First time…well, I've passed through. First time down here.

RUBY: Maybe you didn't know that there are a lot of black people in Cardiff.

CARLO: What's your name?

RUBY: Ruby.

> (*Pause.*
> *They look at each other intensely.*
> *CARLO suddenly bursts out laughing.*)
> What?
> (*CARLO speaks with difficulty.*)

CARLO: I can't…it's just…it's…like two rubber dinghies! Ha, ha! O fucking hell! (*He plays with his lips. Pause. He laughs.*) What?

RUBY: (*Raging.*) Get out! (*Pause.*) Get out!

> (*CARLO suddenly jumps up.*)
> Fuck off!

CARLO: You can't tell me to fuck off! You're in my fucking country! My father was the dictator of Spain!

RUBY: Fuck off back to Spain then!

> (*CARLO takes RUBY savagely by the throat.*
> *RUBY struggles.*)

CARLO: (*Viciously.*) You fucking cheeky, tar-filled black-shelled cunt! I am your fucking master!

> (*RUBY makes choking noises.*)
> I've come across a fucking country for this! Across my country! Mountains and fucking lakes! It was time for the country boy to have his bit of black and now I fucking want it! So this is inevitable. This part of the events of your life is an inevitability! Are you clean?

RUBY: (*With difficulty.*) Leave me alone!

CARLO: Are you clean?

RUBY: (*With difficulty.*) Fuck off!

CARLO: Well let me give you this fucking warning. If I, having fucked the arse off you, catch a foreign black disease and take it home with me to my beloved western fields, I will return with the wrath of a wronged nation and you and all your fucking ape mates'll pay. (*He swings her round and slams her face down onto table top.*) You know? I feel that I have, at this moment, found myself. Found my power and my authority!
(*Lights down.*
RUBY cries out.)

Scene 4

BEN and SERENA sneak on. BEN is a little drunk; giggly. After a moment we can see SION eavesdropping. They speak urgently sotto voce.

SERENA: This is your chance!

BEN: To do what?

SERENA: To get out of here! Leave! Sneak off into the night!

BEN: But I don't want to! I'm enjoying it! It's a good laugh!

SERENA: Jesus!

BEN: You know at the bottom of Bute Street there's a fish shop?

SERENA: Yes.

BEN: I used to deliver there. That's where you know me from.
(*SERENA looks surprised.*)

SERENA: It is! But...(*Pause.*) What's different?

BEN: I had long hair.

SERENA: (*She seems suddenly extremely anxious.*) I do remember you. You always had this grin on your face! You'd pull up, jump out and everybody would be greeting you with warm laughter and back slaps. And you'd unload the fish...and...you've got to go! You don't belong here! (*Pause.*) That person was not a killer. You must go!

BEN: It's alright!

SERENA: It's not alright! (*Pause.*) That's life, isn't it? I wake up one morning, two things on my mind: my mother saying: The west of Wales owes me; and me thinking: I don't belong. I don't belong in this city. It's as if my mother was telling me where to go. So I came west. I escape the city and I find this. This! Can you fucking believe it? I could belong here and what happens? You turn up! As if Cardiff has delivered a rotten kipper to my paradise breakfast!

BEN: Kipper!

SERENA: Go! Leave me, please, to my good luck!

BEN: He wants me to stay. HE wants ME.

SERENA: And what about Sion? The longer you stay the more he'll expect and he won't like being disappointed. And you don't look like a killer to me!

BEN: Who can say what a killer looks like? In a war, your own brother becomes one. Your uncle. The doctor who treats you. Maybe your father is a mass killer. A hero.

SERENA: Why don't you say that you exaggerated? On the spur of the moment. You didn't think. Say Thornycroft was shouting at you, you shouted back, he slipped and banged his head. And that was that.

BEN: Why?

SERENA: Sion feeds off Carlo. Whatever's on Carlo's mind will end up on Sion's only all twisted up and magnified! Your being here is turning Carlo to always thinking about the project. Can't you see this? The project is becoming this uncontrollable thing in Sion's mind! (*Pause.*)

BEN: I'll think about it tomorrow.

SERENA: No! I need this! I WANT it! And I'll do anything to make it work.

BEN: It's making you blind! He's a middle-aged greaseball!

SERENA: You're not going to fuck it up! Go! Now!
(*SION rushes on. He punches BEN in the head. BEN falls. SERENA cries out. SION puts a hand over her mouth.*)

SION: Listen to me you both. You fucking Mick and you fucking nigger. He's fucking in love with both you cunts but I know all about you! He believes in you both and as long as he does you'll fucking live up to it! Personally, I'd prefer it if he saw right through you! (*To BEN.*) You fuck around and I'll gut you and strangle you on your own colon and throw you in Tregaron Bog. You think Carlo's a fucking joke because he's polite and entertains you. Don't make the mistake of thinking that with me. Don't even make the mistake of thinking that about him! (*He lets her go roughly.*)

SERENA: Ben! Are you alright?!

BEN: (*Dazed.*) Yeh.

SERENA: (*To SION.*) You're fucking crazy!
(*SION takes hold of SERENA viciously and pushes her face onto table with his hand over her mouth.*
BEN looks dazed and shocked.)

SION: (*Almost tearfully.*) Before you fuckers came I was his favourite! (*He presses against her.*) Can you feel it hard? You fucking behave or you'll find it in you!

SERENA: (*Breaking free.*) Fuck off! D'you think I won't tell Carlo about this?

SION: I'll say it was an accident!

Lights down.

Scene 5

The same. Next morning.

The table is the same with the map and gauntlets. CARLO comes on. He is wearing the army tunic and a gun in a holster. He sits. He looks at audience. After a moment he smiles broadly at audience. SION comes on yawning.

SION: I need to go to work.

CARLO: You've got work here. The appaloosa! I'm a new fucking man this morning! All geared up for the project! I excelled myself last night!

SION: You don't need me now. You've got him.

CARLO: Christ man! You sound like an unrequited lover! D'you want me to give you a kiss? You're a mediocrity!

So petty! More English than Welsh. You wouldn't dream of doing what that boy has done.
(*Pause.*)

SION: How d'you know he did it?

CARLO: Everybody knows he did it!

SION: Who?

CARLO: The man he did it to knows he did it! *I* know he did it. You know he did it. Serena knows he did it and he knows he did it. Who else needs to know he did it?

SION: That doesn't prove he did it!

CARLO: What the fuck is this? You told me he did it! You believed he did it! What kind of inadequate are you that you don't even believe in your own beliefs? You can't even extend into the world of ideas a belief that is so clearly believable!
(*Silence.*)
Where is he?

SION: I don't know. Maybe he's with her.

CARLO: What makes you say that?

SION: No! It's okay. We'll give him the benefit of the doubt.

CARLO: What doubt?

SION: The doubt about him and what he's going to do.

CARLO: What he's going to do with Serena?

SION: No. What he's going to do with this whole thing!

CARLO: Aha! You think he might be a fifth columnist!

SION: If you mean spy, yes. It's possible. I mean, they're always watching you since you went to jail. You're the most watched man in Wales! That's why everybody who's not one of the watchers loves you.

CARLO: Don't flatter me you fucking lily! For him to be a fifth columnist they would have had to set up a huge detailed operation to plant him! To put him in position. Isn't that right?

SION: Yes.

CARLO: So how would they have done that? You met him down in New Quay making fishing nets. Right? How would he have known that that's where he could meet someone who would know me?

SION: Now hang on, Carlo. Don't forget I was down there because of those bloody...I said it was a conspiracy! What was going on in the dole office? They're the ones who sent me down to New Quay! Don't you think that it's a bit strange that he turns up?

CARLO: Okay. Let's assume that what was going on in the dole office was an MI5 conspiracy... They arranged to get you this job making fishing nets, then they arranged for him to also get a job. So. They've got you together. Now they've got to get you talking. Who spoke first?

SION: Well...I did. I think.

CARLO: Uhu. First point. Second point: do you really think that if they wanted us to believe he's a killer, that they would come up with the story that he told you? That this man killed another man with a fish? Don't you think that that is so far fucking fetched?

SION: Well you believed it!

CARLO: I believed it because it is so unusual! I mean, if he'd come to us and said he'd sliced this guy with a shiv I might not have believed it.

SION: Why?

CARLO: Because that's exactly what you'd expect someone to say if they were an MI5 agent. You can use a man with a shiv. You can't use a man with a frozen fish. Very easily. And, of course, what caps it all is that he took the fuckers head off!

(*Pause.*)

SION: He didn't. I made that up.

(*Pause.*)

CARLO: You made that up?

SION: Yeh.

CARLO: Fine! That's the one bit of the story I didn't believe! Why did you make it up?

SION: Because I wanted you to believe that I'd discovered this fantastic, unbelievable murderer and that you'd think better of me.

CARLO: Uhu, and now you want to believe he's an MI5 mole. Maybe that's because the idea of having Her

Majesty's Secret Service on our case brings some
importance to your otherwise insignificant little life by
association with me and you'll get everybody thinking
better of you! But I don't need it! I don't need the
attention of a foreign power's spy network to know that
I am somebody! (*Pause.*) So if he didn't decapitate him,
what happened? Did he just clout him on the head with
the fish?

SION: Yes.

CARLO: So he did clout him on the head with the fish!

SION: *I* don't know if he did. He said he did!

CARLO: And what happened to the victim?

SION: Well, there was no one else there at three o clock in
the morning so he just made out that he'd slipped and
banged his head! The thing is anyway, if he did kill him
with the fish, did he mean to or was it just an accident?

CARLO: How?

(*Pause.*)

SION: Maybe he lifted the fish out of the box to put it on
the back of his truck and he slipped and the weight of
the fish propelled him through the air and he only
stopped when the fish made contact with the man's head!

CARLO: That would be an accident.

SION: Yes. But that's more far-fetched than what he said
happened.

CARLO: Precisely. All you've done is make me more
convinced than ever that this boy is a great killer with a
dead fish! You come to me first thing in the morning
with your miserable Iago passion, you jealous fucker!
Get out of my sight!

(*BEN comes on.*

SION looks at him suspiciously.)

Ben! Sit down, boy.

(*BEN sits.*)

How is she?

(*BEN looks confused etc.*)

BEN: Well...I...u...who?

CARLO: Serena! Who the fuck else?

BEN: Well I thought…maybe the horse.

CARLO: The horse! You see? He cares about my horse! How is Serena?

BEN: I haven't seen her.

CARLO: Sleep well?

BEN: Yes.

CARLO: Let me ask you something straight. Did you kill the man Thornycroft?

(*Pause.*

BEN looks at SION.)

BEN: Yes.

CARLO: Excellent. What shall we do today?

BEN: I think I'd better go to work.

CARLO: Nonsense. You're working for me now. (*CARLO indicates project map. Pause.*) Project Fuhrer. (*Silence.*) No?

BEN: Are you a Nazi?

CARLO: Me, a Nazi? Do I look like one?

BEN: No. Actually you look more like a Nicaraguan freedom fighter.

SION: He's taking the piss!

CARLO: Excellent! Only remember this: *omnes deteriores sumus licentia!*

BEN: What does that mean?

CARLO: Too much freedom and we become a bunch of twats!

BEN: O.

CARLO: So: the project!

SION: No!

(*Pause.*)

CARLO: (*To BEN.*) Let's confront this head on because we're going into very serious territory. I know we're all sitting here jittery from the extremes of last night but let's focus our minds. This project is something I've worked on for many years. Waiting for someone like you, Ben, to turn up. What we're talking about here among the joking and the fun, is glory. We're talking about the glory of Wales. And also, trust! I trust those who trust me. The people of Wales have invested in me, invested in us – without even knowing it – all their hopes for an English-free tomorrow; a Queen-free tomorrow. A nation with a President. A nation which, one morning in a not-too-distant future – in the early days of our liberation – will begin a new history. The kind of history that Tacitus would write about – a history which is made by us and owned by us. A history which is no longer a sub-species of history – conditional on the English history; decided by English imperialism. A history that defies the mediocrity that history in the modern era – written by the English – has awarded Wales. (*Silence.*) So are you with us? I am committed to you! (*Silence.*) I trust you.

BEN: Why? You don't know me.

CARLO: So tell me not to trust you! One thing about me: I know how people mock me; how your liberal jerk-offs with their cosy democracy which keeps the people out of politics, think I'm a crackpot.

BEN: Not my liberals.

CARLO: But one thing about me: I trust. I trust Wales and I trust Wales to trust me. Can I trust you? (Pause.) I am committed to you! And you? Are you a man who can show commitment?
(*Pause.*)

BEN: Well... That job: the fish delivering. I was as committed to that job as any man could be. Committed to anything. I believe, in the end, I was committed to fishness. A kind of politics: Fishism. I would drive until two in the afternoon and then drink. I'd go with the boys to someone's flat, crash out and be up at eight and in the pub again. Still wearing my fish clothes. In a packed pub I would have room to tango. I smelled like a fucking bream! I didn't have halitosis I had halibutosis. That was my commitment to Thornycroft – I became what he sold! I became so much a part of that fish ethos that I lost my identity. I was a person who worked in the fish industry. I became a fishist! There is no greater commitment!

CARLO: Brilliant! (*To SION.*) What about that?

    (*SION nods reluctantly.*)

    (*To SION.*) And you? Are you committed? Committed enough to stop this fucking bickering?

SION: Aye.

CARLO: Shake on it! The three of us.

    (*The three join hands and CARLO raises them up.*)

    Viva le fucking Revolution! *Salve!* All of us!

ALL: *Salve!*

    (*SERENA comes on. She looks unhappy.*)

CARLO: (*Holding his arms out.*) Serena!

    (*She refuses to look at CARLO.*)

    You look as if you've seen a ghost. (*Pause. He goes to her and holds her tenderly.*) It's an early, crisp, Spring morning. The daffodils are in bloom and the appaloosa is with foal. The successful outcome of that situation is as close to my heart as it is to yours. Isn't it a marvellous thing? The birth of a horse. *Dum vita est spes est.* While there's life there's hope. (*Indicates map with a flourish.*) And close to my mind is this: It's time to initiate Ben into the secrets of the project.

SION: No!

CARLO: I've told you! (*Pause.*) Go to the appaloosa!

    (*Silence.*

    SION leaves reluctantly.

    SERENA sits.)

    (*To BEN.*) Let me show you these places. Lake Vyrnwy, The Alwen Reservoir, Llyn Celyn, Llyn Clywedog. Have you ever seen the film *Chinatown*?

BEN: No.

CARLO: My favourite film. It's about water. Corruption and water. It's a story every Welshman should understand and cherish. In the past we blew up pipe-lines. This time we're going to up the ante! What I want from you is...a kind of trial run. To prove yourself. To yourself. The attack won't be made at one of the more infamous lakes. The attack will be made here at Llyn Brianne. Above Rhandyrmwyn.....

SION: (*Off.*) Carlo! Carlo! (*Comes on.*) Come quick! I think
    she's about to go!
    (*CARLO rushes off.*
    SION pauses, looking at BEN almost threateningly. He picks
    up the gauntlets. He folds up the map and leaves it on the
    table before going.)

SERENA: We've got to go. Now!

BEN: What's happened?

SERENA: I don't want to talk about it. (*She begins to cry*
    bitterly.) He's one fucking seriously sick bastard. (*Pause.*)
    I wanted so badly to fit in here. (*Suddenly raging.*) I've
    told you to go! If you wait any longer you'll have to do
    what he wants. A killing! And you're not a killer! (*Short*
    pause.) Are you? (*Almost attacking him.*) Are you?!
    (*SION is eavesdropping.*)

BEN: No! Okay! I don't know why I ever said it!

SERENA: It was a hustle.

BEN: I suppose so. On the spur of the moment. But why did
    they believe it? I don't even look like a killer! I don't
    think I've ever even hit anybody! Except when I was a
    kid. In school.
    (*SION goes.*)

SERENA: You've got to go!

BEN: I am! Back to my job.

SERENA: What job?

BEN: With Thornycroft!

SERENA: You haven't even left there?

BEN: No! I'm on holiday.

SERENA: And Thornycroft?

BEN: He used to make me angry. I got mostly angry
    because he made me feel so stupid! But the most I ever
    did was shout at my mirror.

SERENA: Shit! That's Cardiff for you! Shouting at mirrors!

BEN: We'll pretend we're just going for a walk.
    (*They leave.*
    SION comes on with CARLO.)

CARLO: That poor fucking horse! She's going to die! Did
    you call the vet?

SION: No.

CARLO: Why?

SION: Because we don't need the vet! We don't want authority people around here. We've got a huge fucking problem that we've got to solve.

CARLO: I don't want to hear this! My heart is breaking over that poor fucking horse!

SION: You can't trust him!

CARLO: I can trust who I want!

(*CARLO opens bottle of whiskey and takes a deep swig. He then opens the project map.*)

SION: But why him?! He's from Cardiff! That's not much better than being English itself!

CARLO: He arrived out of the blue! The blue I watched through my morning window! Just when he was needed. Not just that but...he's Byronic!

SION: I bet Byron was a socialist!

CARLO: He was a fucking Lord!

SION: So why do socialists call their sons Byron? Like Byron Morris? His old man was in the Labour Party.

CARLO: Shut up!

SION: It's almost like vanity! As if you trust him just because he likes you!

CARLO: *Vanitas vanitatum, omnis vanitas!* Everything is vanity. That's what it is to be human! If you think not then you delude yourself and you give yourself a gravity made stupid by the delusion. Think of the appaloosa! Can you? That beautiful creature out there. Her world is one I am so taken with I often live it in my imagination. Just fucking subsume your assumptive pettiness in the collective whinnies of my mare!

SION: That's just a metaphor. He's having a...he's...him and Serena have started something.

(*Pause. CARLO swigs.*)

CARLO: Explain yourself!

SION: She was climbing all over him!

CARLO: Like what! How? How does one climb over another? Watch what you say!

SION: She had her hands on his shoulders.

CARLO: You abnormal swine. They're comforting each other because they're afraid that they may have failed to come up to my expectation!

SION: Why are you being so…so pig-headed and so stupid?
(*CARLO clouts SION.*
Silence.
SION suddenly looks threatening and CARLO backs off a little.)
The very first time I met him we had a conversation like….like a metaphorical one about the colour of blood and he kept saying that Welsh blood was red.

CARLO: It is!

SION: No! But that's another point! The point is he's a socialist.

CARLO: You think I could be obtuse enough to entertain a socialist by default who then goes on to bed my woman? Christ! If I was that incompetent I'd be a socialist myself!

SION: He's not a killer.

CARLO: Not that again!

SION: Shurrup Carlo and listen! He's never killed anyone! He's never even hit anyone except when he was in school! I just heard the whole thing!
(*CARLO sits.*)
He's a fucking fake! (*Pause.*) Listen! You can chew my bollocks off if I'm lying. And it's not all. He's leaving and he's taking her with him. What you looking so shocked about? They're Cardiff scum!

CARLO: Scum?

SION: I'm angry, Carlo, I didn't mean it like that about her. Let's just say that Cardiff and scum go together in my head right now.

CARLO: Listen you cheap fucking sophist! Scum! I've seen you look at her.

SION: (*Threateningly.*) Don't talk to me like that! Are you saying I look at her like that? She's yours! I fucking respect you!

CARLO: (*Jumping up.*) Respect! What would a fucking slave like you know about respect! You're jealous of our Adonis! That's the reality!

SION: I'll get him in here. (*SION comes to front of stage and looks into audience. He points.*) Look! There they are! Leaving!

CARLO: They're just going for a walk!

SION: That is not the walk of a man just going for a walk! That is the walk of a man shitting his pants!

CARLO: Fuck off! The walk of a man shitting his pants is like this: (*Does the walk of a man shitting his pants.*)

SION: No! That's the walk of a man who's already shat his pants! That... (*Points to front.*) ...Look! They're getting further down the drive!

CARLO: Listen you fucking constipated, virginal toady! You couldn't insult me more than to say she has left my home and bed to go off with some cunt from Cardiff! Even a killer and young man for whom in every other respect I have the greatest regard! They are going for a fucking walk!

SION: (*Still looking to front.*) So why are they running?!

CARLO: They're fucking jogging! She's loosening her limbs for tonight!

(*SION runs off.*)

(*Shouting after him.*) There's a horse in real pain out there while you're pursuing this fucking red herring! (*Picks up whiskey bottle and practises swinging it.*) I could do without this! Reality time. Desperate measures. (*Looks into audience.*) They were just going for a walk, now they're really running! Down the drive! That fucking Sion! He's building to something. I should have listened to my mother: beware the hambone with pretensions! Run faster, Serena! Fuck, he's got them! Here it comes. The reckoning. Be prepared for hard times! *Non semper erit aestas.*

(*CARLO positions himself at the table with all the authority he can muster. We can hear shouting off.*)

After a moment, BEN and SERENA are brought on by SION. The three stand before CARLO in silence.)

Ben. *(Pause.)* Be calm. Serena. *(Pause.)* Do you love me? Do you love me Serena?

SERENA: You know....

CARLO: That's enough! That's enough! *(Silence.)* Ben. *(Pause.)* Be calm. *(Pause.)* Can I trust you? *(Pause.)* Can I trust you?

BEN: But...

CARLO: That's enough; that's enough. Let's get straight to the point. Did you kill the fish man with the salmon? I don't mean: did you kill the man who owned the salmon, I mean: did you, with a salmon, kill the man who organised the selling of fish? The man you worked for? *(Pause.)*

Did you?

BEN: No.

SION: Hit him!

(Pause.

CARLO looks at SION with anger.)

CARLO: Shut it.

SION: What're you waiting for? Hit him! He'll wriggle out of it!

CARLO: *(To BEN.)* Have you ever killed a man?

BEN: No.

SION: You don't need any more! Hit him now!

CARLO: I'm trying to get to the bottom of this!

SION: We're at the bottom! There's nowhere lower to go!

CARLO: *(To BEN.)* Have you ever killed anything?

(Pause.)

BEN: I killed a worm once.

SION: He's taking the piss!

CARLO: *(Suddenly exploding, to BEN.)* Don't mock me! *Aut bibat aut abeat.* You're either for us or against us! *(CARLO rants.)* What is it about me that encourages you to think you can mock me with impunity? D'you think I'm an idiot? Do you think...is it my face? Do I look comical? A little anachronistic perhaps: the moustache, the bandana, Franco's tunic? What kind of complacency is it that can encourage you to think that there's no danger in mockery? It must be that under no circumstances could you imagine that I could be dangerous! O I know about your Cardiff and your Saturday nights and how the valley vomits up all its wretched humanity and collects it in the downtown city in the curry shops and scrumpy houses and maybe you think that is dangerous while this…this little life of pastoral calm is for peasants; those close to flowers and grass. I trusted you and you qualified my trust! You decided that this was the trust of a crackpot! That the trust of someone who looked so implausible could be real or otherwise according to your whim! But even if I am a crackpot, even if I am an anachronism aren't I a man? Don't I have the qualifications for friendship?

BEN: You wanted me to kill someone.

CARLO: I was testing you…

BEN: But…

CARLO: Shut up! What about respect! Tacitus said that in the ninth year of the war with Britain the reputation of Caradog 'had spread beyond the islands and through the neighbouring provinces to Italy itself.' To Italy itself! Those words! 'Even at Rome his name meant something'! And he spoke to the whole of Rome from the dais in front of Caligula and Agrippina, he spoke to the world in Latin: 'I had horses, men, arms, wealth. Are you surprised I am sorry to lose them? If you want to rule the world, does it follow that everyone else welcomes enslavement? If I had surrendered without a blow before being brought before you, neither my downfall nor your triumph would have become famous'! He lectured the Romans in their own language and they respected him! And I am mocked by you in my own home in the fucking English language! Don't you think I'm a man? Don't you think I need to be respected? Don't you think I need friendship?

BEN: Yes…

CARLO: Treachery! *Punica fides!*

SION: Hit him!

SERENA: No!

CARLO: Don't you think I deserve some of what was given to Caradog?

BEN: Yes!

SION: Hit him!

SERENA: No!

CARLO: (*To SION.*) Shut up! (*To SERENA.*) What's it to you? (*Silence.*) Has the blaggard bedded you?

SION: Why are you just talking? Why don't you fucking hit him!

CARLO: Shut up! I'm trying to deal with this English fucker!

BEN: I'm from Cardiff!

CARLO: (*To BEN.*) Have you been fucking Serena? Have you?

BEN: No! I admit I didn't take it seriously...but...mean... you believed in the fish! How could I take it seriously? ...if you know what I mean... I didn't even take it seriously that you were some kind of...you know... fascist...Nazi.

SION: Destroy the fucker!

BEN: No! I liked you!

SERENA: Let's just leave it!

SION: Leave it?!

BEN: The thing is...where we come from, Cardiff...none of this Welsh stuff matters. It's a joke! It's like... What's Wales? Wales is a made-up pop group trying to make it big on the Eurovision song contest...

SION: I don't believe I just heard that Carlo! That's a fucking horrible metaphor! De-limb the cunt!

BEN: No listen! Listen...the only fish I knew in Cardiff that's had any kind of connection with fascism is Frankie Fish from Splott – a master with a shiv – you want somebody to be a fascist for you – go to Frankie Fish. Christ, I know...

CARLO: You think I'm not a fascist?

BEN: I didn't say…

CARLO: Answer the fucking question! You don't think I'm a fascist, right? You don't think…

BEN: I think…

CARLO: Don't think I'm strong enough? Mad enough? Think I can't do it?

BEN: DO it?

(*CARLO takes gun out of holster and points it towards BEN madly.*)

CARLO: This gun hasn't been fired since the Civil War! Do you think I can do it?

BEN: Do what?

CARLO: Shoot it!

SION: Do it!

SERENA: Don't!

CARLO: Do you?

BEN: Yes!

(*CARLO is struggling with the gun.*)

SERENA: No!

CARLO: The fucker won't cock!

(*CARLO struggles with the gun. It goes off.*
BEN falls. SERENA cries out.
SERENA falls down beside BEN. SION kneels down beside BEN.)

SERENA: You fucking coward! You fucking mad…

SION: (*To SERENA.*) Shut up! (*To CARLO, looking at BEN.*) You shot him! Looks like he's lost half his head!

CARLO: It was an accident! The gun went off!

SION: The bit below his ear is gone. Shot off!

CARLO: Gone where?

SION: I don't know. Have a look around.

(*CARLO begins to search for the piece of BEN's head.*
SERENA cradles BEN's head.)

SERENA: You're a fucking inadequate!

CARLO: (*As he searches. Excitedly.*) I can't go back to jail, Sion! I can't go back to jail! Say you did it! You say!

SION: Calm down!

SERENA: We've got to help him!

CARLO: (*To SERENA, madly.*) Shut up! (*To SION.*) I can't go back! You don't know what they did to me in there!

SION: What d'you mean? They admired you! They looked up to you! You were their leader! You were everything to them!

CARLO: I'm talking about Swansea jail! They buggered me! I spent nearly eighteen months in solitary! And the Welsh cons were the worst! Snakes in the grass! *Anguis in herba!* (*SION goes to CARLO and now seems to tower over him.*)

SION: When you came out, we began this project. You said, when we're ready we'll have an army. Cons. All we'll need is that special one who you can trust – because you didn't think I was up to it and you couldn't trust the cons.

CARLO: You're going to say you did this. This will be your contribution to the project.

SION: I can't fucking believe this! You're telling me there's no army?

CARLO: Of course there's no fucking army! When are you going to grow up?

SERENA: I'm going to phone for the police.
(*She begins to go.*
SION takes her roughly from behind and holds her tight with an arm around her mouth. She struggles, kicking him etc.)

CARLO: (*Beside himself with fear and rage. To SERENA.*) Do you love me?!

SION: Forget that!

CARLO: I asked if she loved me!

SION: Are you telling me I've wasted all my hopes, all my dreams, all my young-man's-chasing-lifetime on a fucking fantasy?

CARLO: Calm down, Sion!

SION: (*Through gritted teeth.*) No! I may have missed a couple of fucking meetings but I have not missed the plot! I've believed in this! My one belief! And now I find that there's no army! If there's no army and no project, why did you want him? Maybe you're a fucking homo now!

(*SION throws SERENA down and grabs hold of CARLO's tunic in an uncontrollable rage.*
SERENA goes back to BEN.)

CARLO: *O tempora! O mores!* These are bad times!

SION: You let yourself become a bum boy! What kind of animal are you?

CARLO: I am a horse owner and citizen of Rome!
(*SION pulls his head back to head butt CARLO.*)
Civis Romanus sum! I am a Roman citizen! Don't do it!
(*Silence. SION holds the pose for a moment.*)
Morituri te salutamus. We who are about to die salute you!
(*SION spits and lets CARLO go.*)

SION: I'm going to check the horse then you can go fuck yourself.
(*SION turns to go.*
CARLO suddenly springs up, takes SION by the hair at the back of his head and throws him to the floor. He very efficiently takes out a flick knife and opens it. CARLO is astride SION, almost as if he's buggering him.)

CARLO: You think you know me? You think you know when to move against me? You will never hurt me! I have an arsenal of faces. Whatever's necessary to inspire the mob! But you – you have one face and I will mark it!
(*He puts the knife to SION's forehead.*)

SION: No!

SERENA: (*Tearful.*) You're nothing! Both of you.
(*CARLO lashes out and catches SERENA's leg.*
She cries out.)

CARLO: (*To SERENA.*) Shut up you black bitch! Who do you think you are? Don't think I needed you! You're not the only black woman I've had! No! But the other one, she loved me. And she did love me! I remember her draped across an old Victorian bed and I remember thinking: I am Carlo. King of Cardiff, King of the Negroes.

SERENA: They'd make mince-meat of you!

SION: Go on! Slice me! Make me angry! Then let me show her!

81

(CARLO pulls SION's head back and is about to draw the knife across his forehead.)

CARLO: Did you hear that? The horse!

(Lights begin to go down.
CARLO pulls the knife across SION's forehead.
SION cries out.
CARLO rushes off followed by a maddened SION.
Silence.
SERENA remains with BEN.
Sound of a shot gun shot, off.
SERENA gasps and turns to look in direction of shot.)

Lights snap off.

Scene 6

CARLO's home.

BEN is sitting alone holding a cloth to his head. After a moment, SERENA comes on, crying bitterly.

BEN: What was it?

SERENA: *(Through her tears.)* He shot the horse!

BEN: Who?!

SERENA: Sion! Shot that beautiful appaloosa!

BEN: Where's Carlo?

SERENA: *(Sniffing back her tears.)* He's kneeling there beside the horse. Crying. Sion was standing there giving a Nazi salute! *(Pause.)* Are you okay to go?

BEN: Yes.

(SERENA goes to BEN. She takes away the cloth.)

SERENA: In the end, not much more than a flesh wound. Come on.

(They leave. SERENA has an arm around BEN. After a moment, SION comes on carrying a shotgun, a smudge of blood across his forehead.)

SION: The fucker marked me. I let him do it so that he could save face in front of his black whore. He'll never mark me again.

(*Pause. He looks into audience.*)

There they go! Walking down the drive. Hand in hand. Walking not running! Ha, ha! (*Shouting as if to them.*) You can get a bus from here to Cardiff! (*Quietly as if to himself.*) The Traws Cambria. Once a day. Well, twice a day. Goes one way then the other. Crosses Wales. From North to South. Bangor to Cardiff. You can cross Wales in a day. On a bus. Across the zones. The language and people zones. (*Pause.*) The people in the North, we hate them. Arrogant fuckers. Can't stand them. You come south and you hit Machynlleth and then you hit the real zone. Ours. Real people. While you travel through that zone you go through what Carlo calls sub-zones. (*Pause.*) Fucking sub-zones. Lampeter's a zone and Llanybydder's a zone and they hate each other's guts. The only time one lot will go into the other lot's zone is on a Saturday night. For a war. Me and him (*CARLO.*), we're from different zones. The fucker marked me. I let him do it so that he could save face. He'll never do it again. Then you get to Carmarthen and that's the end. Then you get into that whole South Wales valleys shit whatever zone. I wouldn't want to go on that bus. And now look! There they go.

(*Silence.*)

The metaphor is dead!

(*Pause.*)

Lights down.

LOLA BRECHT

a post-modern comedy

for Gwenda

Characters

PETER BRECHT
an evangelical preacher in his forties

LOLA BRECHT
a common woman, his wife, in her thirties

IMRA/IMRI
owner of hotel in Slavkov

NAPOLEON

The set should be minimal consisting only of what's needed:
a chair, a bed, a telephone etc. And in the first scene a sign
saying *Slavkov*, for example. The arguments at the head of
each scene should appear on a large printout or, more
prosaically, on boards.

Lola Brecht was first performed at Theatr Arad Goch, Aberystwyth, on 11 October 1995 in a production by Castaway Touring Theatre, with the following cast:

LOLA BRECHT, Lindsay Blumfield

PETER BRECHT, David Blumfield

IMRI/IMRA/NAPOLEON, Paulinda Knight

Director, Ian Marsh

PART ONE

Scene 1

The argument: BRECHT leaves the train at Slavkov to provoke his destiny.

Slavkov station. Waiting room. A sign saying 'Slavkov' can be seen. There is also a sign saying: Toilets. Sound of a train leaving.

PETER BRECHT, a German, comes on. He is a man of medium build and a strong face of Teutonic set. He carries a travelling bag. He also carries a rolled-up newspaper. He seems at the end of his tether. He stops still holding bag and paper. Suddenly, IMRA comes on from the toilets. She looks crazed. She is carrying an enormous knife with a lot of blood dripping from it. IMRA pauses. She looks at BRECHT in silence. He looks at her with surprising calm. Then he suddenly looks behind him with a momentary panic as IMRA leaves quickly. After a moment, LOLA comes on. She is BRECHT's wife. She is short and almost fat. She is a common woman. She is ordinarily not a pushy woman philosophically or even morally, but now she is very angry albeit in a kind of bewildered way. She too carries some bags. As she speaks she stands behind BRECHT.

LOLA: (*Breathlessly, urgently.*) Are you having a breakdown or what?

BRECHT: Don't be so absurd! You'd know if I was having a breakdown.

LOLA: How?

BRECHT: Because I'd be like this: (*He suddenly drops his bag and acts a breakdown: doubled over, clutching at himself and blubbering incoherently.*) I don't want to…blubber…I can't go on! Blubber, blubber… Life is meaningless…blubber, blubber, blubber…I am an ant…blubber…

LOLA: Just stop it! This is serious!

BRECHT: Is it?

LOLA: You got off the train! Marthe's meeting us at the station in Prague and now the train's gone!

BRECHT: (*Suddenly angry.*) Marthe? Who the hell is
Marthe? Do you think I could care less about Marthe?

LOLA: Who is Marthe? I gave her up for you!

BRECHT: What were you? A lesbian?

LOLA: Shut up, Peter! You know full well me and Marthe
grew up together. We were nurses together. She is STILL
a nurse which I gave all up. I gave up my own mission
to come on yours! You might not be having a breakdown
but now I feel like I am!
(*She drops bags.*
BRECHT sits.
LOLA looks around her confusedly.)
There's no one here! It's as if someone dropped an
atomic bomb that just kills people! I'm going to find out
the time of the next train. Where are we? (*She looks at
sign.*) Slavkov. (*Suddenly wailing.*) I wanted to get to
Prague! And you NEED to get there! Last night
everything was going so well. On the train. You were
flying like a bird – even singing songs! Then this
morning you buy that newspaper and BOOOMMFFF!
Misery! One minute we're on the train to Prague, next
minute you're getting off!

BRECHT: There won't be another train. Today.

LOLA: What do you mean? What did you read in the
newspaper?

BRECHT: The train timetable.

LOLA: Don't make fun of me Peter! They wouldn't have a
train timetable in a paper like *Der Spiegel!* They have
stocks and shares and death letters to famous men. Like
capitalists. (*LOLA pauses. She lights a cigarette.*) I know
what it is. (*She draws deeply on cigarette.*) You read about
Rheinardt Bonnke again.

BRECHT: Bonnke?

LOLA: You told me he was in Prague last week and left.
Why would the world's most famous evangelist not be in
Prague when the rest of you are meeting there? Maybe
he's too famous like some of our playwrights. Maybe
he's above it all!

BRECHT: Shut up, Lola! You're driving me mad!

LOLA: Well you've always been envious of him! Just because he's more famous. But what's fame Peter? You said yourself that fame needs corpses to breathe. By which I suppose you mean it sucks the breath out of living people to glorify the dead! Well you're alive while Rheinardt Bonnke may as well be dead if he's going to be so famous! You shouldn't take it out on me.

BRECHT: Take what out on you?

LOLA: That you haven't got his destiny! You're always on about it...

BRECHT: That's a lie!

LOLA: ...destiny – and yet you're the one who's stopping us getting to Prague!

BRECHT: (*Cruelly.*) Destiny is beyond you Lola. You wouldn't understand it. Prague was just our destination.

LOLA: I couldn't care less! What difference does it make if we're not going to get there?

BRECHT: (*Raving.*) Have I ever forced you to do anything? I didn't tell you to get off the train did I? Why didn't you stay on it? You could have met Marthe without me! (*Silence.*)

LOLA: Maybe I will have a breakdown. And commit suicide. That's what I feel like.

BRECHT: You're a magician! That you can conjure up this despair. It requires a creative energy which can only come out of hatred and frustration – hatred for me; frustration that you have no real identity of your own. It's that capacity you have for quarrelsomeness; for wanting to put things, if I may say so, on a war footing, that caused me to leave the train and abandon my career. (*LOLA snatches newspaper.*)

LOLA: It's in here and I'll find it!
(*BRECHT tries to get paper back.*
She runs from him.
He chases.)

BRECHT: Give it back to me!

LOLA: (*With cigarette in mouth.*) Not yet, Peter! (*She takes cigarette from mouth. She points newspaper at him shaking it.*)

If you want to talk about despair, well you're a writer!
You write sermons!

BRECHT: Yes! But so what?

LOLA: Everybody knows what writers get like – envying
others of their ilk.

BRECHT: Ilk?!

LOLA: You know what I mean! But people like Rheinardt
Bonnke are born with destiny! They're always going to
be famous! Other people are not. The best they can do is
slave away at life's puzzles. Which is why so many
people do crosswords!

BRECHT: (*Snatching paper from LOLA in despair.*) I can't take
this any more! I am going to commit suicide!

LOLA: Don't try and steal my clothes! There's a difference
between an idle threat like yours and my threat which is
just on idle.

(*BRECHT begins to go to toilet. He pauses.*)

BRECHT: Lola, you have no right to speak to me as though
we were on equal terms. Your commonness obliges you
to be ordinary. You can't expect anything from life but
the commonplace. For me, things are palpably different.

LOLA: Where are you going?

BRECHT: (*Impatiently.*) To the toilet! (*Pause. He goes.*)

LOLA: Maybe that's why! The real reason! Because you
wanted the toilet and didn't want to do it on the train!
And all this argument has been a smokescreen because
it's funny how you've gone in there as soon as you got
up as if the movement inspired your bladder. If you
didn't want to go on the train why didn't you say? I'd've
understood. I'm a nurse! I know all the many little
difficulties of the toilet. Was it because the train
MOVES? Trying to be sure you keep it in the pan?

BRECHT: (*Off.*) Shut up, Lola! Shut up!

LOLA: I know of men who can't hit the pan when the
world's quite stable! You should sit down like a woman!
It's not particularly humbling! We have to put up with
much worse!

(*She flicks the end of her cigarette into the toilet and turns
away. BRECHT lets out a cry from off. He comes on. He is
rubbing his eye.*

Pause as LOLA watches him with dread.)
What...what is it Peter?

BRECHT: (*Pitifully.*) Your cigarette end went into my eye.
(*He sits.*)

LOLA: (*Compassionately.*) O, God! O Christ, Peter! I'm
sorry! I'm sorry! This whole vendetta has got me so
worked up and careless! Let me look!

BRECHT: Leave it, Lola! Leave it!

LOLA: Leave it? How can I leave it, I'm not a leaver! (*She
falls to her knees before him.*) O, let me look, Peter! Did it
go right in? Could have burnt the bloody iris! I'm so
sorry Peter! So sorry!

BRECHT: Leave it Lola! I'm alright!
(*He pushes her.*
She gets up.
He takes out handkerchief. He puts handkerchief to his eye.
LOLA stands wringing her hands.)

LOLA: (*Tearfully.*) I am without ANY kind of destination. I
can see that. Having a destination gives you the reason
for the things you do. IT MAY BE JUST GETTING TO
A DOOR! I don't even do the things I should any more!
I've even lost the rudiments of nursing. In my time I've
cared for humanity in the whole gamut from bringing
babies into life to cleaning up the semen of crazed old
men. Now he takes out his own handkerchief and places
it on his eye. I am the person who burnt his eye. Maybe
if I stop smoking that will be a destination. Maybe if I
make this effort TO STOP SMOKING so that I burn no
more eyes, that IT will be a destination. Do you think,
Peter? Do you think if I make this effort to sort my life
out that you can forgive me? That you can set me on the
road that will give my life some – I don't know –
meaning?
(*Silence.*)
I'll leave you alone. For a minute. I'll go to the toilet
myself. I may as well. Now that we're here.
(*She goes off to toilet.*
BRECHT takes a sneak look in the newspaper. He stifles
a cry and crumples the paper. After a pause he tidies paper.

LOLA comes on. She looks in a state of shock. She stands still in silence for a moment.)

Peter, there's a body in the toilet.

(*BRECHT puts a handkerchief back to his eye.*)

BRECHT: What do you mean?

LOLA: There's a body in the ladies' toilet.

BRECHT: What sort of body is it?

LOLA: A body! (*Pause.*) A dead body.

BRECHT: (*With handkerchief to his eye.*) I think I meant... Well I don't know. It raises so many questions. Like, I suppose, is it a man or a woman?

LOLA: I should think it's a woman in a woman's toilet.

BRECHT: But did you see it?

LOLA: No, it was stuck behind the door.

BRECHT: (*Getting up.*) Are you sure you're not misunderstanding things?

LOLA: I'm not.

BRECHT: It could be a delusion.

LOLA: What?

BRECHT: You could have imagined it.

LOLA: But I didn't!

BRECHT: It may be something else.

LOLA: Like what?

BRECHT: I don't know. (*Pause.*) It seems...fantastic. Absurd!

LOLA: Go and have a look!

BRECHT: No! (*He makes a big thing of his eye.*) I'm not in a fit condition.

LOLA: But there's a body in the toilet and you're a Christian! Don't you think you should...BLESS it? It's dead with maybe a soul hanging about in that disgusting place waiting for someone like you! If it was only wounded I'd do something with my nursing skills. Go in!

BRECHT: No!

LOLA: But I want you to know that I know what I saw!

BRECHT: But you don't!

LOLA: Will you go?

BRECHT: NO!

LOLA: Why?!

BRECHT: Because it's a ladies' toilet! I'm sorry Lola, I'm not prepared to go into a ladies' toilet on a wild goose chase! (*BRECHT picks up bags and begins to go off.*) We need to find somewhere to stay overnight. I'm going to find a hotel.

LOLA: I want to wait in case there's another train.

BRECHT: (*Angrily.*) I told you! There's not going to be another train!

LOLA: Well how do you know? Did God tell you?

BRECHT: Don't be so unnecessarily irreligious. If I may paraphrase you, Lola, you're the one who's always on about destination. Don't you think we should arrive somewhere? There is no purpose in waiting for something that won't come.

LOLA: But what about the body?

BRECHT: If there IS a body, do you think it's any concern of ours?

(He goes.

She stands in silence for a moment looking after him then picks up her bags and follows him off.)

Lights down.

Scene 2

The argument: BRECHT uses his moral authority in pursuit of his destiny; LOLA is crushed beneath its weight.

Hotel room. Chair, bed, mirror, window, telephone.

BRECHT comes on, followed by LOLA. He seems more confident. She looks worn out. BRECHT stops, drops cases and turns to her.

BRECHT: (*Impatiently.*) Death is like birth. You can never satisfactorily investigate it. When a child's born, it's because two people have had intercourse. Would it do you any good to dig into the, by definition, distasteful details of an intimacy you weren't a party to, to understand the child?

LOLA: You seem more relaxed. Must have been the walk from the station.

BRECHT: Not at all. I feel more...determined.

LOLA: To get to the bottom of things?

BRECHT: No. Precisely NOT to get to the bottom of things. Not to jeopardise the child's innocence by worming around in the muck of the act that gave him his existence, if there was a woman and she was dead, we couldn't know how it happened and it would do us no good to try and find out.

LOLA: But she was left so casually. There were bullet holes. She had slumped against the door. I saw blood beneath the door!

BRECHT: Bullet holes? You said nothing about bullet holes!

LOLA: I've just remembered.

BRECHT: Yes, yes, Lola. Very convenient.

LOLA: I'm worried! I did see the blood!

BRECHT: Far be it from me to bring up women's matters, but you should know women DO bleed, Lola!

LOLA: I do know! I do know that!

BRECHT: It's not for me even in this post-feminist world to preach to you, I know, about your predispositions...

LOLA: You mean periods?

BRECHT: If you must...

LOLA: But I'd know if there was menstrual blood! I'd know!

BRECHT: No you wouldn't! You COULDN'T! No one knows about what they didn't witness! Did you, for example, see an alternative hole in the woman for the effusion?

LOLA: I couldn't see! I couldn't get the door open! She was stuck behind the door. D'you want me to show you how I think she might have been? (*LOLA gets into a position which would describe a woman who has been shot in the head and fallen against a door so that her blood drips from her head down the door.*) You see? Here's the door. (*LOLA puts a hand flat against her forehead.*) If she's shot in the head the blood would drip down the door and form a pool. Her bottom is over there. (*She indicates.*)

BRECHT: But you just said you couldn't get the door open to see!

LOLA: Yes.

BRECHT: So her bottom could have been there where your head is!

LOLA: But how?

BRECHT: Well, like this of course!

(*BRECHT gets on his hands and knees. He indicates his bottom to show where door would be.*
LOLA gets up.)

LOLA: I would have seen her feet beneath the door! (*Gently kicks his feet.*)

BRECHT: You wouldn't... (*Bends his knees and lifts his feet up.*) If the feet were pressed against the door.

LOLA: Look at your head! Look where your head would be! Her head would have been in the pan!

BRECHT: So what? She wouldn't know that that's where her head was if she was dead! It's not something she'd be doing out of choice!

(*Silence.*)

LOLA: Well, anyway, I think you've introduced this crude element just to win the argument. But we can all be crude.

BRECHT: Crude?

LOLA: Yes. And for all I know you don't really know anything about a woman's body at all.

BRECHT: (*Hurt.*) Of course I do!

LOLA: For all I know, you probably think that her vagina is a slit in her belly!

(*BRECHT gets up indignantly.*
Silence.)

BRECHT: That's cheap!

LOLA: Why?

BRECHT: Because if it was the case I would have said that it would have dripped into the middle of the floor!

(*Silence. BRECHT brushes himself off.*) I DO know about

97

a woman's body, Lola, but I cannot say that I know the cycles of a woman's mind! What the explanation is for that woman's body being in that position in that toilet anyone may guess at but I don't believe that she was murdered.

LOLA: At least you seem to be accepting that there WAS a woman's body in there.

BRECHT: (*Sighing.*) O have it your own way but what good will it do you?

LOLA: I'm going to look for a bathroom. (*Puts case on bed and looks out of window.*) Look at that Peter! Isn't it spectacular? And look at that building. We'd have to watch nobody sees us...um...undressing. They could see from there! Right into this room! Should we draw the curtains?

BRECHT: No. Enjoy the view.

LOLA: It must be the best room in the hotel!

(*LOLA goes.*
BRECHT makes an obscene gesture to her back. After she's gone he looks at himself in mirror. He takes off his jacket and tie and looks at himself again and sighs despondently.
There is a knock.)

BRECHT: Yes?

(*IMRA comes on. She is dark – Turkish looking. She's carrying some towels.*)

IMRA: I've brought some towels.

(*BRECHT looks at IMRA in silence.*)

I'll put them on the bed. (*She goes to bed in silence. She places towels carefully on bed. She seems to be building up to saying something. She stands before BRECHT. They look at each other in silence for a few moments. They speak at the same time.*)

BOTH: You...

BRECHT: You first.

IMRA: You don't seem surprised.

BRECHT: Surprised?

IMRA: That it's me. (*Pause.*) Don't you recognise me?

BRECHT: O yes. I was going to say: you don't seem perturbed.

IMRA: About what?

BRECHT: About it being me. (*Pause.*) I can understand.

IMRA: Understand?

BRECHT: There's a war on isn't there?

IMRA: How do you know about the war? It only started yesterday.

BRECHT: So there is a war?

IMRA: Yes.

BRECHT: Where is it? (*He holds his arms up.*) It's so quiet!

IMRA: People are keeping their heads down before the onslaught. Today I think it's over in Havel's field. In fact I know it is.

BRECHT: How do you know?

IMRA: My husband is commander of the troops that support the German declaration of support for the independence of our enclave, Slavkov. To be known as the Independent Democratic and Indivisible Sovereign State of Austerlitz.

BRECHT: Yes. Slavkov used to be known as Austerlitz. I read about it on the train. But it's a big name for a mere enclave. Isn't it? Or is that the point?

IMRA: What?

BRECHT: Please. Won't you sit down?…Um…what's your name?

IMRA: Imra. I'm sorry. I have to go.
(*IMRA goes.*
BRECHT stands alone. He seems a little stunned.)

BRECHT: (*To himself.*) Imra, Imra. (*Pause.*) Imra.
(*After a few seconds there is a knock.*)
Yes?
(*IMRA comes on.*)

IMRA: Why did you get off the train if you knew there was a war on?

BRECHT: Destiny?

IMRA: Destiny? Are you a German?

BRECHT: Yes. And you? What…a Turk?

IMRA: No. I am a German.

BRECHT: You don't look like one.

IMRA: I married a German.

BRECHT: Of course! Your husband. The commander. Is this why you gave us this room? It must be the best room. With such a view.

IMRA: Yes.

BRECHT: Because we're German?

IMRA: Do you want to fight?

BRECHT: I don't know. The reason I got off the train...it was, I suppose, impulse...a sense of something. It's as if I felt that if I could experience something of the suffering, it will add meaning to my ministry. I suddenly envied you your war! YOUR destiny!

IMRA: (*With some impatience.*) Destiny?!

BRECHT: I'm a...I'm an evangelical preacher...

IMRA: Like Herr Bonnke?

BRECHT: Of course. You know of Herr Bonnke?

IMRA: Yes. He gave a sermon. It started our war.

BRECHT: But is that really the case?

IMRA: Yes. The Neo Christian Right Wing Government in Berlin was encouraged to recognise our enclave by Herr Bonnke's sermon. Where were you going when you got off the train?

BRECHT: To Prague.

IMRA: Holidays?

BRECHT: No. I was to give a sermon at an evangelical convention.

IMRA: You were going to an evangelical convention in Prague even though Herr Bonnke has left there?

BRECHT: Well...

IMRA: He passed through here last week after starting our war. He is a hero to us.

BRECHT: (*Suddenly very uncomfortable, even angry.*) O yes! And what a responsibility! But where is he now? That's why I got off the train! I will say, I find it a little shabby that someone can so casually create a DESTINY for a nation – albeit an enclave – one that will no doubt rub off on him, and then calmly leave it to fend for itself!

IMRA: I must go.

(*IMRA leaves quickly.*

BRECHT paces. He is in turmoil. He seems annoyed with himself.

A few seconds later, there is a knock.)

BRECHT: (*Impatiently.*) Yes?!

(*IMRA comes on.*)

You!

IMRA: Herr Bonnke has a saying when referring to those he would save: it is – from the guttermost to the uttermost.

BRECHT: I know it.

IMRA: This beautiful little war is his.

BRECHT: I know! I know!

IMRA: (*A little angrily.*) Perhaps you have a saying for us. A motto?

BRECHT: I'm sorry. You must be angry. All I was saying was: where is Rheinardt? Why isn't he here?

IMRA: Where is Rheinardt? That is your motto?

BRECHT: Well…no…well…

IMRA: Yes! It's good!

BRECHT: Very well, then: where is Rheinardt?

IMRA: I suppose he's too busy.

BRECHT: Was Napoleon too busy to fight the Battle of Austerlitz? Having started the war?

IMRA: Then perhaps you are the man and not him!

BRECHT: (*A little puffed up.*) Well! Let us at least say: I am available!

IMRA: You can help, Herr Brecht.

BRECHT: You know me?

IMRA: Yes. The register.

BRECHT: O. Yes.

IMRA: I have a brother Imri. He's on the other side. He is very hostile to all that is German. It's in the way he speaks and in the way he walks. I mean, when he speaks German he speaks with an un-German accent DELIBERATELY; when he walks, he walks like a slave DELIBERATELY bent over – to be provocative, anti-German. He has classic resentment. We want – my husband and myself and all those who welcome the support of the Germans, to be bold and independent like the Germans. But he, Imri, my own brother, wants us held back in this Federation with our neighbours which has run its course. My brother has become an anti-German terrorist.

BRECHT: Terrorist?

IMRA: Yes. Yesterday this was an extremely busy hotel. The lobby was full throughout the day with people who had fled the fighting. Others were simply on holiday when the war started. Imri began identifying those who were pro-German to terrorise them.

BRECHT: (*Appalled.*) What do you mean 'terrorise'?

IMRA: Doing whatever he feels needs to be done. Didn't I see your wife in the corridor?

BRECHT: It's possible.

IMRI: She should be warned. She is precisely Imri's kind of target.

BRECHT: (*Suddenly panicky.*) O no! No! She must not be told about any of this! About the war!

IMRA: Why?

BRECHT: Why? I have to live with her! She'd be impossible, Imra. She used to be a nurse. She thinks she has that healing touch. She'd be like a one-person peace-keeping force. She'd make your life a misery!

IMRA: Then you'll have to deal with Imri direct.

BRECHT: What should I do?

IMRA: Perhaps you can begin by using your moral weight.

BRECHT: Moral weight! Yes! (*Pause.*) Yes. (*Pause.*) God, yes! This is it! I'm so glad I've met you Imra! I mean I am SO glad. Can I...will I see you again?

IMRA: Of course! I'm here. In the hotel.

BRECHT: About your brother: should I go to him? Should I look for him? What does he look like?

IMRA: I think you were right. I think you were born for this. He'll come to you. I feel sure. He looks like...well, he looks like me!

BRECHT: When he comes to me, will he come...to hurt me?

IMRA: Are you afraid?

BRECHT: A little...a little fear and trembling perhaps.

IMRA: Let me see.

(She takes BRECHT's hand. She holds it tenderly between her two hands. They look at each other in silence for a moment. They let go of hands as LOLA comes on. She's carrying a book.)

LOLA: O.

BRECHT: Lola, this is Imra. She...she...

IMRA: It's my hotel.

LOLA: O well. I found a bathroom. It's very nice...

BRECHT: This is my wife, Lola.

IMRA: Hello. *(Shakes LOLA's hand.)*

LOLA: The wallpaper in the hallway is very...I don't know...Russian? Oriental? It sets the tone. I might look for some like it when I get home. And the taps and the other fittings must have cost a lot. Of course, you wouldn't think of expense in a hotel. Even though it's not very busy. I could hear some sounds in the distance. Out in the night. Like small explosions. What could it be? I found this book. About the battle.

BRECHT: What battle?

LOLA: That Battle. The Battle of Austerlitz.

BRECHT: O.

(BRECHT holds his hand out.
LOLA hands him the book.
He gives it a cursory look and hands it back.)

IMRA: I hope you'll be comfortable.

LOLA: Yes.

BRECHT: Yes. I'm sure.

(IMRA goes.
LOLA suddenly slumps onto bed. She begins to cry.)

LOLA: O, God, Peter! We've got to get out of here! I really don't want to face what I just saw!

BRECHT: Saw?

LOLA: I just saw, I just saw...no, I can't say it. It was awful. I can't say it to YOU...

BRECHT: Say it, Lola.

LOLA: No. I can't!

BRECHT: I'm commanding you to!

LOLA: I just saw a woman with a man's penis...

BRECHT: I don't want to hear this!

LOLA: ...in her mouth! But it wasn't natural.

BRECHT: You think I, a Christian, wouldn't know that?

LOLA: No. I mean she didn't want it. I'm sure!

(*Pause. BRECHT holds LOLA.*)

BRECHT: Why won't you let me help you? Your need is my need. But what purpose does it serve to drag me into a fantasy world in which I can be of no help! In which you deny me that need?

LOLA: What are you talking about?

BRECHT: Lola, I've been watching you. I've seen this development. It's deeply worrying. Is it my fault? Have I cared for you so well – mollycoddled you – to the point that there seems to be little if any purpose left for you? It's as if you search for meaning in irrelevancies about décor or relating to me things that haven't happened.

LOLA: It happened! It happened. (*Gets up.*) I'll tell you ALL that happened. From the beginning. Then you'll see I Couldn't possibly have made it up.

(*BRECHT puts his head into his hands.*)

I walked down the corridor. There are lots of doors. I don't remember so many doors. I was looking for one that might have a word on it. Bathroom. I would pass a door and hear a whimper as though a dog was recovering from a battering...

(*BRECHT begins to chant to himself a prayer, maybe the Lord's prayer.*)

I found the door. The door I was looking for. I opened it because it was unlocked. There was this woman. And she wasn't naked or anything: not slim or svelt, just an ordinary peasant woman; a chambermaid or something, on her knees as if she was praying. She didn't look sexually aroused or anything as far as I could tell in the split second I saw it. I didn't see too much of the man at all.

BRECHT: What did he look like?

LOLA: I'm saying I don't know. Swarthy. Dark.

BRECHT: Like a Turk?

LOLA: A bit.

BRECHT: Like that Imra?

LOLA: Imra?

BRECHT: The owner.

LOLA: A bit, I suppose. Yes. I have to admit I seemed riveted to that one snapshot. I didn't understand it. At first. I suppose to see them fully dressed with just this one bit of flesh protruding...but then, I must have seen it all and yet if I saw it all why would I think it was all in her mouth? (*Short, short pause.*) Obviously because it was going in and out! She was just kneeling there like a woman at her prayers! I hardly saw the bathroom! (*LOLA falls to her knees beside bed.*
BRECHT kneels on bed holding LOLA's head.
As she speaks, building to a crescendo, he lets out evangelical howls and delivers his lines with an evangelical awe.)

BRECHT: Lola, I'm fearful for your mind! You must step back from the brink!

LOLA: She was kneeling there like a woman at her prayers and it was him! He was the one going in and out! O, God, Peter! Don't you know what that means?

BRECHT: No!

LOLA: It means she was having her face raped! In and out, in and out! And there's something else now I'm thinking of it. There was something on it! On his penis! Do you know what I think it was? And this is coming right off the top of my head but it just reminds me of something I remember in hospital among some of the young men, the young patients during a time when tattoos became very popular, especially in rare places, I think it was a snake. I think the man had a snake tattooed on his penis. And do you know why I think this? Because just for the briefest instant, the head came out of the mouth and there on the head of the man's penis was what I'm sure looked like a snake's head. And this is because I've seen a snake's head on a man's penis before.

BRECHT: For God's sake Lola! You poor, sad, creature!
Don't you think every woman has that fantasy?

LOLA: But it must have been a tattoo because otherwise
why would his penis have looked like a viper or is it
possible that it's just me being poetic? No, no! I don't
think so. The fact is, if it wasn't a tattoo it would have
meant that the man had a severely bruised penis and how
could any man get such a bruised penis and still want to
use it in outrages?

BRECHT: (*Shouting.*) No, no, no Lola! THIS is an outrage!

LOLA: It was just going in and out in and out of the head of
just an ordinary innocent woman! He was torturing her!
(*Silence save for LOLA's sobbing.*)

BRECHT: Lola, I pity you. (*Silence. BRECHT gets off bed
and sits in chair.*) Your life is a grey morning. A grey sea.
A grey seal beached on a colour denuded grey beach. A
grey car. A great grey limo of a car. Empty. Your life,
Lola, is a great grey empty limo of a car. As you open
the door and go in you see that all the upholstery and
interior decoration has been slashed and ripped. People
have vomited and bled over the seats. There may be
used condoms or discarded knickers. Initials and hearts
have been carved half-heartedly in the walnut. And once
you're inside you realise the true context of the grey car.
It's in a scrapyard! You look out and all you see are
scrapped vehicles. Some of which, maybe, embodied
dreams. Some took people on holidays. And before your
eyes from the back of your dead limo, you see a great-
claw take up these little worlds on wheels and drop them
into a machine in which they are crushed and out of
which they emerge meaningless blocks of steel. It's no
wonder you search so desperately for signs of life,
because that's what your stories of death, violence and
sex are, Lola: a search for signs of life! Meaning! But I
won't let you drive me to despair with your pathetic
quest to bring meaning to a meaningless life! All you've
described is two people having sex! Jesus Christ, it's a
hotel!

(*Pause.*)

LOLA: I may have been describing someone who could murder a woman in a toilet. (*Silence. LOLA gets up. After a moment she turns away from him. She goes to lock the door.*) I don't think anything would be beyond that man. (*She goes to sit.*) It's getting dark. (*Silence.*) I'm going to read this book. (*She sits.*) Calm down. Lose myself in a bit of history. Will you go out after and look into the bathroom for me? Make sure it's not just a shower. A woman should soak.

Lights down.

Scene 3

BRECHT goes to war!

The Argument: BRECHT is drawn further into IMRA's plotting that puts LOLA at the mercy of history.

The same. Later.

BRECHT is at door shouting to off.

BRECHT: Have a good soak!
(*BRECHT is barely into the room when IMRI rushes on. He is, of course, the same person as IMRA. The long hair of IMRA should be tucked into a cap like a guerrilla might wear. He speaks with an accent but not a German one. IMRI is holding a gun which he immediately points at BRECHT.*)
(*Shocked.*) No! Don't shoot!
(*BRECHT puts his hands up.*)

IMRI: Afraid?

BRECHT: I know who you are!

IMRI: And I know who you are! Brecht. A German. You've come to steal my country!

BRECHT: I haven't!

IMRI: You have! You Germans believe it's your destiny to control the whole of Europe! Only not by conquest. No! The Post-Modern Age: by recognition! Recognise this enclave as Independent states, start little wars and move into the devastation that results. You want our destiny.

BRECHT: No, please! Let's get this straight! Like any man I want A destiny, yes! But on an individual level. Like you, I dare say.

IMRI: I may but I don't want a German destiny. A German destiny for someone who's not German, especially at a time when the Germans are in a mood for destiny is not a good idea.

BRECHT: But do you think that the Germans are in a destiny mood?

IMRI: Your Herr Bonnke has said so.

BRECHT: He's not my Herr Bonnke.

IMRI: But you're an evangelical preacher like him aren't you? Albeit an unheard-of one. He started this war! Which you, no doubt, have come to gloat over. Anyway, down to business. You've got a wife haven't you?

BRECHT: Yes.

IMRI: A fat woman.

BRECHT: Well...fattish.

IMRI: Shall I tell you what my intention is? I'm going to do her.

BRECHT: Do her?

IMRI: I'm going to rape her.

BRECHT: Is there...is there anything I can do?

IMRI: Do?

BRECHT: To help. I mean to help you not do it? Could we reach an arrangement?

IMRI: Christ, man! This is war not a game of strip poker! I'm going to FUCK her. Pervertedly!

BRECHT: I must object.

IMRI: Why? You brought her into the war!

BRECHT: It was an accident.

IMRI: When I've raped her I'm going to shoot her.

BRECHT: Good God!

(*IMRI appears to be getting tired. He changes his gun-hand but lazily as though deliberately giving the impression that it could be quite easily taken from him.*)

IMRI: Like I shot my sister.

BRECHT: What?!

IMRI: I shot my sister. After I found out she'd been to see you and had told you about me.

BRECHT: But how could you have known that?

IMRI: I asked her.

BRECHT: And she told you?

IMRI: Yes.

BRECHT: And then you shot her?

IMRI: Yes.

(*BRECHT writhes with his hands still in the air.*)

BRECHT: O, God! What kind of people are you?

IMRI: I left her in the hallway. Dying. Bleeding to death. Which is where she will be now unless she's dragged herself off.

BRECHT: How could you have done that?

IMRI: How could you have recognised our enclave?

BRECHT: But I didn't! I never recognised it!

IMRI: (*Very angrily.*) But you've come here to take advantage of the war consequent on the recognition of our enclave by the rest of your Germans beginning with Herr Bonnke!

(*Almost as a reflex, IMRI lashes at BRECHT with the gun and catches him on the face.*

The gun falls out of IMRI's hand.

BRECHT picks it up and immediately begins to pistol whip IMRI.

IMRI cowers and cries out pathetically.

BRECHT is mad as if he were having a breakdown.)

BRECHT: Bonnke, eh? You think Bonnke is big? A hero? You've sold your souls to Bonnke. He gives you delusions! The man's a millionaire! Doesn't it irritate you that in the modern world the heroes of the poorest are the richest? Kids in shanty towns throughout the world with no shoes, no food, no nuthin as they say, have worshipped Presley, Madonna and Michael Jackson. And Rheinhardt Bonnke! He's come into Eastern Europe because he saw a vacuum. He saw that the whole population has been left standing – naked from the waist down. Men have lost their pants and women – their knickers. You may be familiar with the dream.

IMRI: No, no! Please, stop!

BRECHT: Of course, in the dream, the vulnerability of standing absolutely naked, commingles with a wish – the wish that someone will take you and put your genitals in his mouth! All that's happening here is Bonnke's interpretation of a standard dream. The people want their genitals in the mouth of a messiah! What does it mean? Why are they lost upon the plains of changing empires? Where is that constancy? That one solid fact that pins it all down? God and the meaning that God brings! It's Bonnke and Bonnke's God! Only I can tell you. Bonnke won't give them the meaning they need! What do YOU want? Bonnkism? A millennium of Bonnkist values? Why aren't your people turning on him and saying: who do you bloody well think you are? We've got Greek Orthodoxy, Islam, Roman Catholicism, why should we want your Germanic born-again Bonnkism? Why do YOU want Bonnke? Who are your people? They're not German!

IMRI: (*Crying pitifully.*) No. They are the non-Germanic people of the enclave.

BRECHT: So why should you want Bonnke?

IMRI: I don't! I only mentioned him because he started the war!

BRECHT: 'Started the war'! Big deal! I'm up to here with it! Bonnke goes to Prague and everyone wants to go to Prague! Well I'm glad I got off at Slavkov! I, in contradiction to the current trend – the fashion of the day – do not want to go to Prague though all roads may lead there! Yes! So Bonnke would have it! All roads lead to Prague. What's the point of an enlarged Europe if we can't get to Prague! 'Lord, Lord! We need free-running roads coming to the stadium' – this is what they would have said before he made THAT speech in THAT stadium! 'We're only asking Jesus Christ to stop all the confusion and destruction. Free-flowing traffic! No traffic light problem! 'Come on! Come on Imri! Pray with me! More prayer for the roads! 'Father! In Jesus' name we ask thee for free-flowing traffic on the roads into Prague! In fact, I pray, WE pray that on the news tonight it will be reported that this was one of the most traffic-free days of the year'! Pray with me Imri! 'No danger!'

(*BRECHT presses on IMRI's head.*

IMRI's head is in BRECHT's groin.)

Pray! No danger for Bonnke! Pray!

IMRI: (*Tearfully into BRECHT's groin.*) But Bonnke's been and gone and there's a war! Stop hitting me!

BRECHT: Gone! Yes! And now there's a war and I welcome it!

(*BRECHT picks IMRI up and holds him by the collar. They are face to face.*)

I welcome it because if I can't be at God's right hand down here then maybe I can be at it up there! Don't you think war and death are the great comforter for those who fail to make their mark? Think of all those who only pass through Slavkov because they think they're too big for it and then me who they thought had been left behind like someone unwanted on a platform looking longingly after the departing train. I am saved! I don't need my profile in Der Spiegel because I am quite prepared to go out into the square at Slavkov and die in a brutal war!

IMRI: Don't shout in my face!

BRECHT: (*Shouting in IMRI's face.*) Don't shout in your face?! You put your blubbering face in my room you blubbering bastard! Your very presence is a shout to me! Bonnke shouting! Don't shout in your face? You shot your fucking sister! (*BRECHT hits IMRI who falls to the floor.*) And I'm going to find her!

(*BRECHT leaves taking the gun. After a moment, LOLA comes on wrapped in a bath towel. She is drying her hair with another towel which covers her face so that she can't at first see IMRI.*)

LOLA: I made a quick exit, Peter! I'll tell you about it. You'll have to get my clothes. I was reading the book about Napoleon's Battle of Austerlitz – which I've had to leave behind… (*LOLA almost falls over IMRI. She sees him and gasps.*) Who are you?

IMRI: I'm Imri.

LOLA: Imri? But what happened to you?

IMRI: Your husband hit me.

LOLA: But my husband is a noted preacher.

IMRI: He seemed to me more like an Obersturmfuehrer.

LOLA: But why did he hit you? Where is he?

IMRI: I came to tell him…to warn him…

LOLA: Warn him?

IMRI: To stay away from my sister. He's gone to look for her.

LOLA: I'm sorry I'm not following this. Who's your sister?

IMRI: Imra. You haven't met her? She runs the hotel.

LOLA: O yes. She was in here earlier. She brought towels. Let me wipe your face. I'm a nurse. (*LOLA helps IMRI up from the floor and sits him on bed. She sits next to him and begins to wipe him with the bath-towel around her.*) I didn't understand about my husband. Why did you say he's gone after your sister?

IMRI: He's in love with her. (*Silence.*) Your husband is in love with my sister. It's dangerous. My sister's husband is a soldier. Heinrich. He's a mad-man. They call him mad Heinrich.

(*LOLA stops wiping IMRI. She goes to a bag and takes out cigarettes. She returns to bed, sits next to IMRI and lights up a cigarette. She inhales deeply. She is very distressed.*)

LOLA: I was going to stop smoking. It was to have been a new destination. And now, once more that destination has been altered by my husband's destiny. I'm smoking too much. Twenty a day I'm up to. I can feel it in my chest. I'm smoking too much. I know that. It's the nurse in me. (*She inhales deeply again.*) I MUST be smoking too much. I can feel it burning my lungs. That's a funny thing to admit to isn't it? Burning you own lungs. As if you turned a flame thrower on yourself. There you are. That's life. My life anyway. (*She looks closely at IMRI and wipes him again.*) I think it's because we're not as close as we used to be. That's why he's shown an interest in your sister. Do you feel better?

IMRI: Yes.

(*Pause.*)

LOLA: But it doesn't make sense! Do you think he knew her before? Is that why he got off the train? That would make sense. He said that I'd taken away his destiny. Perhaps he knew her before he knew me and that by marrying me he lost her and has come back now to...to...to be honest I don't want to think about it. (*Pause.*) What a mess. (*Pause.*) I had hoped for so much. Happiness. A child. CHILDREN. A nice home. Nothing too exceptional. That would have been my destiny – if that's what it would have been!

(*Pause.*)

IMRI: Am I wounded?

(*LOLA looks closely at IMRI's face.*)

LOLA: It's nothing much. Thankfully it's superficial. But you have a mark on your face. That will be there for a while. To remind you of my husband. (*LOLA is touching IMRI carefully, gently wiping his face etc.*) This Heinrich. He won't hurt Peter will he?

IMRI: He is a soldier. It would mean nothing to him to kill your husband.

LOLA: KILL Peter?! O God! (*Pause.*) Do you know Heinrich well?

IMRI: He is my brother-in-law.

LOLA: Have you ever seen him...this will sound impertinent but...well...naked?

(*Pause.*)

IMRI: It's a strange question.

LOLA: It sounds...awkward, dirty but...well there's a long story behind it. (*Pause.*) I need to know if he's got a snake tattooed on his...um...his penis?

IMRI: I don't know. I'm sorry.

LOLA: Only I saw a man raping a woman in this hotel with a tattooed penis.

IMRI: It must be Heinrich! Your husband has put your life in jeopardy. If Heinrich finds out about your husband and my sister then I'm afraid I think he'll come for you.

LOLA: (*Fearfully.*) Me?! But why me? O God, no!
(*IMRI puts an arm around LOLA to comfort her.*)
Will you help me?

IMRI: As much as I can. To me you seem to be at the mercy of histories.

LOLA: What do you mean?

IMRI: Well, there's your husband's and then there's Heinrich's. These histories are not kind. To make Napoleon historical, millions died. How many would die for you?

LOLA: I don't want any to die for me! I'm a nurse not a queen.

IMRI: But do you think history will leave you alone? You're threatened by history. History is like a monster who waits in your corridor. Just outside your door. Sometimes he comes at night and takes you while you sleep.

LOLA: (*Nervously.*) You're having me on.

IMRI: He overwhelms you. With his influence. Like a succubus. You wake in the morning sweating. You're afraid he'll reject you. You look down the corridor for him. You want to at least see some signs of celebration. You want to see people fall at his feet knowing that you and he are one. You may even wish to go to these people and pick one or two and kick them in the teeth. Pull their eyes out. To please him. Or even, if it were possible, take a machine gun and shoot them all. He is the meaning of existence. You want to be his confidante. You'll do anything. You would do anything in front of all these people. Take your own flesh apart before them if necessary. If it will bring companionship. But you look down the corridor and it's empty. Still. You become afraid. What if this was it? What if all were dead and

gone? How could you on your own, alone, without his
help, without even the opportunity to express your value,
or the fact of your existence by shooting or maiming or
by whatever way suits you, exterminating others, how
could you, alone in that empty corridor, that PASSAGE
OF TIME that's going nowhere, carry the proof of even
your existence let alone IMPORTANCE, let alone
SIGNIFICANCE, let alone being ANYTHING but the
fodder for endless volleys that day after day year after
year harvest the millions living to be buried only with
their UNIMPORTANCE, their UNKNOWNESS. You
don't want this. You don't want to have to even worry
about the possibility of this.

LOLA: (*Tearfully.*) No I don't but I think I will now! O my
lovely Jesus! What can I do? Help me!

IMRI: You must be strong.

(*LOLA suddenly throws her arms around IMRI's neck. She
still has the cigarette which burns IMRI.*
IMRI lets out a cry.)

Ow! Ow!

LOLA: What?! What is it?

IMRI: You burnt me with your cigarette!

LOLA: O, no! No! I'm sorry! O, God! Christ! Why? Where
is it?

IMRI: (*Putting a hand to his ear.*) My ear.

(*LOLA jumps up. She is panicking.*)

LOLA: But you see? There's no ashtray! I don't want it to
be like this! I don't want my life to be made significant
by a bad habit, the consequences of which can't be
known simply because there aren't put in place the
ashtrays that are there to let you think of bigger things!
(*Tearfully.*) And I don't know what to do with my
cigarette end!

(*IMRI goes to LOLA.*)

IMRI: It's alright! It's alright! My ear is alright! There must
be somewhere we can put your cigarette.

LOLA: Yes, but where?

IMRI: Give it to me.

(*LOLA gives cigarette to IMRI.*)
I'll take it away.

LOLA: No! Don't go! We'll find somewhere here!

IMRI: No, I'll have to take it. There is nowhere here! I'll come back.
(*IMRI goes.*
LOLA sits despondent and sad.)

Lights down.

Scene 4

The Argument: BRECHT humiliates LOLA and sinks into darkness. LOLA begins to see the light.

The same. A little later.

LOLA is laying on bed still in the bathrobe. There is a knock. LOLA gets up.

LOLA: Who is it?

BRECHT: (*Off.*) Me!
(*LOLA goes off to let BRECHT in.*
BRECHT comes on. He has a plaster across his nose.
LOLA follows him on.)
Thank God you're safe Lola!

LOLA: Why shouldn't I be?

BRECHT: Well...no reason. Except...we're among foreigners.

LOLA: What happened to your nose?

BRECHT: I...um...I was um...I um...I was um...I...you've got blood on you.

LOLA: It's nothing. What about your nose?

BRECHT: It's nothing. What about your blood?

LOLA: I'm not interested in my blood. I'm interested in your nose.

BRECHT: Lola! You may not be interested in your blood but what do you think that means?

LOLA: Means?

(*As he speaks, BRECHT paces wildly.*)

BRECHT: You can't be cavalier about your blood! Even a cavalier if he gave his blood would give it for a cause. A cause to which the blood related. Not a blood relative. That's only a euphemism anyway. Blood belongs to God. Not to relatives. You have it on loan. As if you'd got it from a blood bank. But it's not a co-op bank. You don't have the right...you wouldn't think you had the right would you, to share the blood from God's bank amongst your relatives? Next, you'll be advocating or anyway condoning the depositing of Aids in blood banks by homosexual men in the early 1980s.

LOLA: Me! I wouldn't say that! I wouldn't say they did it! Let alone advocate it! I'm a nurse!

BRECHT: What right do homosexual men have to deposit ANYTHING with God?

LOLA: Shut up, Peter!

BRECHT: Homosexual men have made God turn on humanity! 'I gave you blood and what did you do with it?' He asks. You put a homosexual germ in it! There's only one thing worse than a homosexual, Lola, in God's eye – I don't mean that the homosexual is in God's eye, of course, there is only one thing worse than a homosexual in God's eye and that's a homosexual germ!

LOLA: Don't speak to me like this! (*Silence.*) Are you alright?

BRECHT: Good God, it's nothing! A scratch!

LOLA: I mean...I mean these awful mad things you're saying! Where have you been?

BRECHT: I went to look for you.

LOLA: That's not true!

BRECHT: What?

LOLA: You went to look for that Imra.
(*Pause.*)

BRECHT: Well actually, you're right! I was feeling hungry. I thought: what I'd love now, I'd love a lightly toasted crumpet with just a thin smearing of unsalted butter, a little apricot conserve and a pot of tea for one. So I

called but no one answered the telephone. I had to go
out. No one was coming here. No one was summonable.
O God! That is so sad! No one was summonable! (*Sits.*)

LOLA: Stop it Peter! You're getting yourself in a state! It's
your nose. It's understandable. An injury to the nose can
be depressing. I've seen bigger men than you brought to
their knees by their noses. I worked in a ward where
there are scientists, philosophers, academics of all
persuasion and who do you think made the most noise
coming out of the anaesthetic? The rugby player with
the broken nose!

BRECHT: I went out. Out of the room. Into the corridor.
The corridor seemed endless.

LOLA: Like time?

BRECHT: What?!

LOLA: Time.

BRECHT: Be careful! Be careful of every word you use! Do
not use words without deliberate choice. They are not to
be confused with something you might pick up on the
street. In the gutter. But yes. Like time. I went down the
corridor and passed, incidentally, your bathroom.

LOLA: My bathroom?

BRECHT: It's just a way of saying it. Of course it's not
yours.

LOLA: I meant: the bathroom I was in?

BRECHT: Yes! Clearly!

LOLA: Were you aware of me within?

BRECHT: Yes I was.

LOLA: In what way?

BRECHT: In what way?

LOLA: In what way were you aware of me? You would be
aware of someone if they were singing. For example.

BRECHT: Yes. You would.

LOLA: But I wasn't singing.

BRECHT: No. (*Pause.*) I went down the corridor into the
lobby. There was no one there. I walked across the lobby.
A man carrying a tray like that...(*He suddenly jumps up*

and imitates a man walking quickly with a tray held at face level.) …came out of a room and walked straight into me. (*Pause.*)

LOLA: And the tray hit you on the nose?

BRECHT: Evidently. I collapsed. I must have been unconscious. I woke in a room. With this plaster on my nose. They must have facilities for dealing with injured guests. Is it your blood? (*Pause.*) O well! What does it matter where the bloody blood came from?
(*Pause.*)

LOLA: It's all over your face.

BRECHT: What is?

(*BRECHT feels his face guiltily.*)

LOLA: That you love her.

BRECHT: Love who?

LOLA: That woman Imra.

BRECHT: Are you insane? (*Pause.*) Now I understand! This is what you've been building to! You create, with your fantastic stories this ambience of sex and depravity to make it POSSIBLE that I could go looking for a strange woman who I barely know so that I can declare my love to her! Or something.

LOLA: Just tell me Peter that you didn't go to look for her for…well because you love her.

BRECHT: I went to look for her for a crumpet! I told you! (*Silence.*) Alright! I'm lying! I did go because…I went because someone had said that there'd been an accident. An accident with that young woman and I went to see if there was anything I could do and if I couldn't to come back here and report to you so that you might go and help by using your nursing skills. That's why I went. (*Pause.*) Now tell me this: what made you think AT ALL that I'd been to look for Imra. Or whatever her name is.

LOLA: Her brother told me. Imri. He told me.

BRECHT: HE told you?

LOLA: Yes! I came in here and found him on the floor where you'd knocked him down. Hit him. Beat him up.

BRECHT: Yes, I did. And do you know why?

LOLA: No.

BRECHT: Because he said he was going to rape you.

LOLA: Rape me? Don't be so stupid, Peter! Why would anyone want to rape me?

BRECHT: He is a terrorist!

LOLA: A terrorist?!

BRECHT: That Imra told me. His own sister told me that he's a terrorist! He's probably the one responsible for the so-called murder in the toilet and, if you're to be believed, may even have a snake on his penis!

LOLA: But this isn't true of that Imri.

BRECHT: Aha! Now then! Why would you be defending a terrorist whose clear intention was to rape you, unless he actually did it and you let him?

LOLA: (*Outraged.*) O God, Peter! How could you say something like that?

BRECHT: Lay down Lola. On your belly. On your belly on the bed.

LOLA: What? Why?

BRECHT: Because I want to look up your vagina!

LOLA: (*Disgustedly.*) My vagina? But…but why?

BRECHT: Because I want to see if he's been there!

LOLA: That's disgusting! You're the one who's always going on about being a Christian.

BRECHT: (*Pompously.*) A little more than that I fancy! I'm a proselytiser.

LOLA: What's that supposed to mean?

BRECHT: (*Impatiently.*) I'm a converter! I convert people from one thing to another.

LOLA: You mean like you want to convert me into a dog?

BRECHT: Just do it Lola!

LOLA: No!

BRECHT: I'm your husband! I have every right to look up your vagina! (*He manhandles her and rolls her onto her belly on the bed.*) You will do it! (*In order to hold her down he has to sit on her head. He does this but realises he's not facing the right way. LOLA is struggling, spluttering etc. He turns around holding her down as he does. He pulls her robe up revealing her buttocks and then realises that he still can't see what he wants to.*) Lola. There is a more dignified way to do this.

LOLA: There is no dignified way of looking up a woman's twat, Peter! It's altogether an undignified thing to do!

BRECHT: You could at least keep this decent with your tongue!

LOLA: Alright! Do it! Do it because you'll never have another chance!

(*BRECHT gets off bed.*
LOLA lays still on her belly.
BRECHT picks up her robe gingerly and looks for the briefest instant with a grimace and lets it drop again.)

LOLA: Go on then!

BRECHT: I've seen all I need to see.

LOLA: Examined it?

BRECHT: As far as I need to.

(*LOLA sits up.*)

LOLA: You didn't! You didn't do it! All that rigmarole was so that you could have your own way! That's all! What kind of twisted up person are you? I'm going to get my clothes! I'm sleeping in that bed tonight and you're not!

(*LOLA goes off.*
Almost immediately, IMRA comes on.
When BRECHT sees her he gasps with happiness.)

BRECHT: You're alright!

IMRA: Except for this on my face.

BRECHT: What happened?

IMRA: Imri shot at me.

BRECHT: He shot at you?

IMRA: Yes. Fortunately the bullet only nicked my face. He could have shot my head off.

BRECHT: He shot at you! He did! O God you poor thing. Let me look. (*BRECHT looks at the mark on IMRA's face. He touches it gently then kisses it.*) Let me forever take responsibility for this little profound mark. (*He hugs IMRA.*
She returns his hug.)

121

God! I didn't believe him when he said he'd shot you and now here's the mark to prove it. O God, Imra, I see all the horror, shame, hurt and at the same time determination to fight tyranny, the tyranny of self-obsessed men in that scar.

IMRA: You're being romantic. I understand. It's the war.

BRECHT: O, Imra, no! It's you! You make me romantic!
(*They hug and kiss.*)

IMRA: I want you.

BRECHT: (*Barely audibly.*) What?

IMRA: I want you! Now!

BRECHT: Me? But...!

IMRA: Lock the door!
(*BRECHT goes to lock the door.*
IMRA goes quickly to the bed.)
Come! Come on!
(*BRECHT goes to bed. IMRA draws him onto bed. They make love. As they make love LOLA is knocking at door etc.*)

LOLA: (*Off.*) Peter! Let me in!
(*BRECHT and IMRA continue to make love.*
LOLA's knocking gets louder.)

BRECHT: O God! It's my wife! I find this...inhibiting!

IMRA: Just keep doing it! Do you want some help? Put that shaft so far up me I can feel your balls. I want you to come so deep in me I can taste it!

LOLA: (*Off, shouting angrily.*) Okay! What am I supposed to do? Is this my home from home or what? I'll have to dress out here and go and find myself a cup of tea, I suppose! Or coffee!
(*BRECHT climaxes on 'coffee'.*
Silence.)

IMRA: O God! Now I feel terrible!

BRECHT: What? What is it? I feel so good! So free! I haven't felt like this for so long. Because I haven't done THAT for so long!

IMRA: I feel guilty. So guilty. I have betrayed Heinrich! Can you say a prayer for me?

BRECHT: Yes. But what sort of prayer?

IMRA: A prayer asking forgiveness. A prayer that says this never happened.

BRECHT: But it did! It was...it was beautiful!

IMRA: O don't be absurd! Don't you know what will happen now? Your wife will find out.

BRECHT: But how?

IMRA: Because you will tell her. If you are the honourable man I think you are. You won't be able to go on living suppressing it. Then she will tell Imri.

BRECHT: But why should she tell Imri?

IMRA: Because it will be a way of placating him. Of distracting him. Of preventing him from raping her.

BRECHT: Well if he was going to do that he would have already done it. He was here.

IMRA: Did he rape her?

BRECHT: She said not.

IMRA: Then they are in each other's confidence! So she'll tell him anyway! Once Imri knows he'll tell Heinrich and then Heinrich will kill me. After he's killed me he'll kill you and Imri will then kill your wife.

BRECHT: But why if she's his confidante?

(*IMRA lifts her arms as if to say: 'There's a war!'*)

IMRA: Why not? There is a war!

BRECHT: O yes. I see.

IMRA: I must go now. To my husband. We will never see each other again.

BRECHT: No! Don't say that! I can deal with Imri! I have a gun! I'll stop him!

LOLA: But even if you stop Imri, what about your wife?

BRECHT: It's alright. I'll deal with her too. (*Sits on bed in despair and holds his head.*) But if I manage to deal with Imri and Lola, there's still Heinrich! Where will it end? And the war! I feel as if...my mind is exploding! Stay! Don't leave me!

IMRA: I can't!

BRECHT: I know. You see? That's my point!

IMRA: What about your destiny? You still have that.

BRECHT: Huh! My destiny.

IMRA: Isn't that why you came here? To find a destiny?

BRECHT: I may have stopped here to avoid a destination.
Prague! But did I stop to find a destiny? I don't know.
Yes. I wondered: why should Bonnke have it all. I am
tortured by his success! It's not fair! He started a war!
He's world famous! Can you believe it? To start a war
and affect the lives of maybe millions forever! There is
no greater destiny! He'll be remembered in history
books. For ever! It's made him a kind of god. Success
can always find a father; failure is an orphan. That's why
you find me lost, wandering in this hostile world. (*Pause.
Suddenly.*) But now I have found a destiny! You!

IMRA: No! It's over!

BRECHT: (*Tearfully.*) No, Imra! Don't say that!

IMRA: I must go! I must!

BRECHT: (*His face distorted with pain.*) Fucking hell, Imra!
Don't go!
(*IMRA goes.
BRECHT returns to bed. He cries.
After a moment, LOLA comes on. She is carrying the book
about Napoleon.*)

LOLA: Peter?
(*BRECHT looks up.*)
Have you been crying?

BRECHT: Crying?

LOLA: Yes.

BRECHT: No, no! I fell asleep. I've been yawning.

LOLA: It must have been a big yawn. Your face is soaked.

BRECHT: (*Suddenly erupting.*) So what! So what! What's it
to you? What if my face was a lake? Why do you have
to be always so bloody pedantic?

LOLA: Pedan…

BRECHT: And sanctimonious!

LOLA: Sancti…

BRECHT: All this damned DAMNED nursing repartee!
All this CARING!

LOLA: You're ill.

BRECHT: ILL?!

LOLA: Ill! You're ill!

BRECHT: You see? Ill! Ha, ha! Bollocks! It's bollocks!
(*Dances around. He is waving his arms in the air. Singingly.*)
It's bollocks! All bollocks! Bollocks and lips of fanny!

LOLA: Why did you lock the door?

BRECHT: (*Stopping.*) Because I um...I was...um...I don't
know! DEPRESSED! Tired? Ill!
(*LOLA goes to bed.*)

LOLA: You've had a woman.

BRECHT: Where?

LOLA: You've had a woman. Here on this bed. I can smell
her!

BRECHT: SMELL her? Smell what? Let me smell! Let me
share it! Let's all have a sniff. Ha, ha! What bollocks!

LOLA: I can smell sex!

BRECHT: You can smell sex? Well let me tell you, Lola!
That's quite another kettle of fish because I too can smell
that. As I dozed off my head fell into the very THICK
of it! But that smell is YOUR smell woman! You
wouldn't recognise it, of course, because, as they do not
say of a fox, one cannot smell one's own hole. But I
know the smell of your hole and that smell is the smell
YOU made with that Imri!

LOLA: You're not going to foist this off on me, Peter! I'm
getting a much clearer picture of things. Imri's made it
quite clear to me that you knew Imra before. And
THAT'S why you got off the train! And another thing: I
went down into the lobby and there are some dead
people there. How come when I go down not long after
you there are dead people there whereas when you went
down there there's no mention of any. All you mention is
a waiter – strolling around with a tray. When I asked
people what's it all about they said that there's a war. You
didn't mention that. So I don't believe you went to the
lobby at all. I think you went to that Imra's room
SNIFFING after her and her husband Heinrich who is
in this hotel – I've got that on good authority – caught
you and punched you on the nose!

125

BRECHT: I know your game! You invent a war to divert
our attention from the fact that you've been having it off
with that bloody Turk. It's the book! You've been reading
about Napoleon's battle and feel confident enough to
make up your own! (*He looks up and speaks as in prayer.*)
Am I less than frank with you Lord? Less than fair? Less
than humble? I'm fully aware of the relationship between
war and sex: the figurative relationship. This woman
can't see it but she's fallen into the trap of her own
metaphor. Blood, war, blood, sex, bed sheet, sex bed
sheet, blood, sex, war. I know what this means. (*To
LOLA.*) I know what this means, Lola! I'm inadequate!
That's what you're trying to say! Isn't it? I'll be frank. I
have a penis THAT'S IN THE SERVICE OF GOD. I'm
sorry if you feel a little...sidelined by this. I don't know
FULLY what it means. I didn't WILL my genitalia on
myself. I had no choice. But if you think I'm going to
use them like an oar is used on a punt then YOU'RE
GOING TO BE DISAPPOINTED! And if it confuses
you, just think what a circus I'm in! Every Messiah,
every evangelist, every disciple, apostle, Pope, vicar,
pastor, parson, cleric has this...this difficulty! The
difficulty of his GEN-I-T-A-L-I-A! And you...you want
to condemn me for taking mine seriously! I'm going to
find that Imri, Lola, and if I don't drag him in here by
his DICK I will apologise.
(*BRECHT rushes off with gun held high. LOLA lays on
bed.*)

Lights down.

End of Part One.

PART TWO

Scene 1

LOLA's dream.

The Argument: Men of destiny discuss the ins and outs.

The same. Later. It's dark outside. Room lights are on. LOLA is laying on her bed asleep. BRECHT comes on stealthily in his underclothes. He is followed by NAPOLEON. BRECHT indicates LOLA to NAPOLEON. NAPOLEON takes off his coat a little ostentatiously. He sits on edge of bed and drops his trousers. Then he realises he hasn't taken his boots off. He sits and tries to take his boots off. After a moment of trying he turns to BRECHT who comes to help him. They make a lot of noise grunting and groaning etc. LOLA 'wakes'.

LOLA: Who is it?

BRECHT: Me.

LOLA: Is someone with you?

BRECHT: Yes.

LOLA: Who?

BRECHT: Only Napoleon.

LOLA: What, THE Napoleon?

BRECHT: Yes.

> (*LOLA lifts herself a little. BRECHT is over the leg of NAPOLEON but the way they're moving suggests to LOLA that NAPOLEON is buggering her husband. She lays back down.*)

LOLA: Now I understand so much.

BRECHT: (*Struggling with NAPOLEON's boot.*) About what?

LOLA: About why you haven't been able to make love to me.

BRECHT: Well. What is it? What is it…bloody hell!

LOLA: Do you have to do it while you're talking to me?

BRECHT: Go back to sleep love.

LOLA: Peter, there's nothing WRONG with loving men.
      And if you'd told me it would have made me feel better.
      Would have made me feel less inadequate.

(*BRECHT lets out what sounds like an orgasmic cry and finally has the boot off.*

LOLA turns away so that she has her back to the two.

BRECHT takes up the same position for the second shoe only now IS moving as though he's being buggered.

LOLA is rolling around feverishly without looking at them.)

BRECHT: THIS is easier. It must have been greased.

(*LOLA lets out a cry.*

Suddenly BRECHT is standing holding the second shoe. Everything freezes for a moment.

This is broken when NAPOLEON speaks.)

NAPOLEON: Suffering means nothing.

(*NAPOLEON is sitting on the edge of the bed while BRECHT sits in a chair.*

LOLA is now laying back comfortably with her head turned towards the other two.)

BRECHT: That's interesting.

LOLA: My husband is a man of destiny.

BRECHT: S-s-s-h, Lola. You embarrass me.

LOLA: Well it's true.

NAPOLEON: War is a sexy game.

LOLA: What?

NAPOLEON: The man domesticated by peace is a frustrated warrior sucking on the woman's breast in her world. He awaits any opportunity to break out – as in war – and investigate the vaginas of foreign women.

BRECHT: How often do you do it?

NAPOLEON: What with other women?

BRECHT: Well I was thinking just – how often do you do it. Full stop.

NAPOLEON: If I'm with the same woman, not every night. In fact, on a campaign NEVER with the same woman. If I'd wanted that I'd've stayed at home.

(*NAPOLEON gets onto the bed so that he's between LOLA's legs. He pushes her legs up and puts his head between them. Meanwhile, BRECHT lays on his side of the bed propped up on an arm watching in a relaxed way. BRECHT and NAPOLEON speak while NAPOLEON is kissing LOLA on the belly, top of the legs etc. The exact nature of this activity is masked by LOLA pulling a bed sheet over things.*)

BRECHT: So. Is the war going well?

NAPOLEON: I think we're getting somewhere. Mmmm.

LOLA: (*A little breathless.*) Do you mean towards a destination?

BRECHT: Of course not, Lola!

NAPOLEON: I mean, we're winning. Last night we took the Pratzen Plateau. (*NAPOLEON has kissed his way up to LOLA's arm. He begins to give her a love-bite.*)

LOLA: What are you doing?

NAPOLEON: Giving you a love-bite.

LOLA: On my arm?

NAPOLEON: Do you have a preference?

BRECHT: Stop being so sanctimonious Lola!

LOLA: No. It's just that it's a strange place to do it. (*To NAPOLEON.*) And I remember reading how you were born with teeth.

BRECHT: So what

LOLA: Well have you ever heard of a baby born with teeth? But Napoleon was.

BRECHT: No! I mean: so what if he was?

LOLA: Well...one might think he might use them. To bite with.

BRECHT: A love-bite is a suck not a bite!

LOLA: I know that, Peter! It's just that most men would suck a neck or a tit and you automatically wouldn't expect those parts of your body to be bitten. Whereas people DO bite arms.

BRECHT: No they don't!

LOLA: For God's sake Peter! They would be more likely to bite an arm than a tit!

BRECHT: You're just being petty! This man has taken a plateau and you're quibbling about where he sucks a bite out of you! (*To NAPOLEON.*) Was it easy?

NAPOLEON: What?

BRECHT: Taking the plateau?

(*During the next speech, NAPOLEON's activities lead him to bury his head deep into LOLA's groin. The speech will have to be made with him coming up for air.*)

NAPOLEON: O yes. I put Legrand's boys on the right – that was my line of battle; the rest of the army I put on the centre and on the left. Just before the battle, I told them: 'While they march – to my right, they present to me their flank!' ha, ha! Isn't that a great line?

LOLA: If by 'flank' you mean arses then it is quite witty.

BRECHT: Lola! Always the COMMON woman. (*Pause. To NAPOLEON.*) You know, you look like that Imri.

LOLA: He looks like that Imra too.

BRECHT: Good God, I think he does!

NAPOLEON: My great master-stroke was to be delivered against the Pratzen Heights by my centre! (*About his activities with LOLA.*) Mmmmmm, mmmmm! Yummy. Christ, I love this!

(*LOLA gasps.*)

BRECHT: What happened then?

LOLA: O, Peter, do you have to?

NAPOLEON: Well, the enemy first attacked in three columns which moved down from their bivouacs behind the Pratzen Plateau towards Tellnitz and Sokolnitz. Then the Austrian advance guard engaged us in Tellnitz but we held up and then they threw the lot at Legrand. God! YUMMMMMYYYYY-O! (*Pause.*) Meanwhile, in the middle, they were all over the place. Utterly disorganised. The line of march of this column was crossed by Leichtenstein's cavalry moving in the opposite direction and they didn't even see it! A gap was created and I sent in St. Hilaire's division towards the plateau. Kutusov was chasing St. Hilaire when he was suddenly confronted with the advance of Soult's men on the plateau itself! Only, there, I had double the force of the enemy! We took the plateau! Not without a struggle but we took it! MMMMMMMM!!!!

(*LOLA's pleasure is building. NAPOLEON almost charges her groin with his head.*)

BRECHT: How much of a struggle was it?

NAPOLEON: (*A little irritated. The following comes out in an impatient flood.*) St Hilaire's right centre division was fiercely engaged by Kolowrat's column, General

Miloradovich opposed the left centre attack under Vandamme, but Vandamme and St. Hilaire are two of my best generals! The rear of the Russian Second column weren't yet committed to the fight on the Goldbach and they made a counter stroke against St. Hilaire's right flank but were repulsed and Soult turned to relieve the pressure on Davout by attacking Sokolnitz! The Russians in Sokolnitz surrendered while an opportune cavalry charge further confused the enemy left and the plateau was mine! MINE!

(*LOLA is panting and convulsing.*)

LOLA: Peter! Am I having a baby? Peter!

BRECHT: What?

LOLA: (*Almost hysterical.*) I'm going to have a baby!

BRECHT: (*Matter-of-factly.*) Then you need to breathe calmly. Calm down. Stop all this convulsing!

(*LOLA tries to breathe regularly but is almost choking.*)

NAPOLEON: What's going on?

BRECHT: She's giving birth.

NAPOLEON: (*As though spitting out something.*) Good God, man, that's bloody vile! Uuuuurghhh!

(*LOLA begins to shout and convulse. BRECHT holds her down at the shoulders.*

NAPOLEON pulls at something between LOLA's legs. He produces an automatic pistol.)

NAPOLEON: (*Marvelling.*) What's this?

BRECHT: Um...it's a pistol. Alright, calm down Lola, it'll soon be over.

NAPOLEON: A pistol?

BRECHT: Yes. An automatic by the looks of it.

NAPOLEON: Automatic? You mean it shoots itself?

BRECHT: Not quite.

NAPOLEON: It's so streamlined!

(*LOLA cries out and convulses again. NAPOLEON pulls out a bayonet.*)

NAPOLEON: A bayonet!

(*LOLA convulses again and cries out and NAPOLEON pulls out a small machine gun.*)

Well, well! Look at this!

BRECHT: It's a machine gun.

NAPOLEON: A machine gun?

BRECHT: Gives off rapid fire. Can kill a whole line of men in a few seconds.

NAPOLEON: O God! I want one! I want one!

(*LOLA cries out and convulses again.*)

LOLA: Is it a girl?

(*She convulses again and NAPOLEON pulls out a severed head.*)

Is it my child? My child? Let me hold it! Let me hold it!

(*NAPOLEON hands her the head in a rather cavalier way. She looks at it and lets out tortured scream.*)

Lights snap off.

Scene 2

A long night's journey into day.

The Argument: BRECHT's arrival at his destiny, puts LOLA in view of her destination.

The same. The moment after the end of Scene 1. LOLA wakes with a gasp. BRECHT is sitting astride her. He has the gun between his legs with its barrel in her mouth.

BRECHT: (*Madly.*) You think we have to believe in something? Like getting to Prague? Well Bonnke's already been there! Bonnke is a success! I'm a failure! There is no God! How could there be a God who would want Rheinardt Bonnke to bring the kingdom of heaven to the Steppes? It's all a pipe dream, Lola! There's nowhere to get to: neither God nor Prague. There is nowhere to get to on this earth! Get to Prague and you'll see. Go on beyond Prague. Cross mountains that you will climb after seeing their summits against the blue interminably blue sky, cross wooded valleys with their innumerable uncountable places each of which might contain a question or, perhaps a lost tribe. Cross desert, seas and on and on, encounter the great cities, parliaments and on and on up the great rivers into hearts of darkness into the improbable core where answers have teased history, where the question can still only be tentatively put and on and on and have nights in Delhi, Djakarta, San Fransisco: drive across America, out-of-this-world experiences, things to last you a thousand lifetimes, cross the white endless, endless snows of Canada and Greenland, Greenland! And finally, finally you will come again to Prague! You may even pass through Slavkov! That's what I can't stand, Lola! I can't stand it! The only destination there can be for man is heaven and that's the only destination you can't know about! We just have to believe it. We just have to believe it's there. Trust! Christ! Why should we trust a God whose greatest gift to us – our power of thought – holds us hostage like a gangster: tells us we're going to die! Our murderer! Isn't that so cruel? And how he enjoys it as he makes clowns of us – the greatest minds are the greatest clowns! Put to use to find ways to justify dying – for the old man who passes away, passes away where? In his sleep! He won't pass Prague! No one passes anywhere and the young man murdered in a war that achieves nothing. It's just commerce. Everything. Going round and round endlessly. Killing is commerce. We kill to keep things going round and round because if we don't we may think we can get somewhere. We may think that a particular war will end all wars. We may believe in destination. But in this world, in this life there IS no destination! Destiny is all we can hope for. And when we find there IS no destination and our fear and trembling won't stop but shakes us to our marrow, we will yearn for wars and DESTINY! Destiny is the substitute for the impossibility of destination! It's that or suicide! We can't keep in this little temple (*Points to his head.*) the Arc of the Covenant. And if it was in Prague we'd have to pass it by! It's there, that's all, just there. Because if it's there, in Prague, and you decide to pass on its side and go in search of what it might mean and go on and search and trek through hell to get there, you will come again to Prague and there it will be. The Arc will be in Prague! And that will be the meaning of the Arc of the Covenant: that it is in Prague!

(*Silence. BRECHT rushes off madly again brandishing his gun.*)

LOLA: (*Shouting after him tearfully.*) Where are you going?

BRECHT: (*Madly.*) I'm going to find out the times of the trains! Ha, ha!

(*In the next moment, IMRI rushes on.*)

IMRI: They've taken the station!

(*Silence.*

LOLA looks at IMRI in shock and bewilderment.)

You won't be able to leave! The people who support the German declaration of support for the independence of the enclave have taken the station! That means you won't be able to leave Slavkov by train!

LOLA: Did you see my husband?

IMRI: No.

LOLA: Then you didn't tell him?

IMRI: Tell him what?

LOLA: What you just told me! About the station!

IMRI: No.

LOLA: And he's gone to the station! (*Pause.*) O I don't know what's happening! He had a gun stuck in my mouth! It's all the stress of being a missionary! He ran off. Said he's going to check the train times. He made love to your sister in this bed and I...I fell asleep in their...stench. It brought on the worst dream I've ever had. And yet he's gone off to get the train times! This must mean that he's left your sister! That he's repented. His sticking that gun in my mouth was a sort of cockeyed way of saying sorry. He's a proud man. He couldn't just come out and say it.

IMRI: Don't be so fucking stupid!

LOLA: But you can't speak to me like that! No woman should have to be spoken to like that by any man!

IMRI: He didn't leave my sister! She chucked him out!

LOLA: Out of where?

IMRI: Heinrich's in the hotel. She's not going to take the chance on getting caught with a man with no future like your husband when Heinrich is such a man of destiny!

LOLA: There's that word again. I don't believe you.

(*IMRI gets increasingly angry.*)

IMRI: Why are you here? In this hotel?

LOLA: You know why! Because we got off the train.

IMRI: Why?

LOLA: Well...I don't know! He said it's because of my quarrelsomeness. But I don't remember quarrelling! It's more likely to be because of something he read in the paper.

(*LOLA is getting increasingly distressed.*)

IMRI: You see? You're a fool!

LOLA: What?

IMRI: What about my sister? He got off the train because of my sister. You told me this yourself. He made love to her in your bed! Don't you think that's O so very German?

LOLA: To be honest, it seems more Italian.

IMRI: (*Pacing. Increasingly agitated.*) He got off the train to meet my sister which in itself is bad enough isn't it?

LOLA: Well...

IMRI: Isn't it?

LOLA: (*A little tearfully.*) Yes!

IMRI: Yes! He got off the train to meet my sister KNOWING that there was a war going on!

LOLA: How do you know that?

(*IMRI picks up paper.*)

IMRI: It's in the newspaper! (*He opens newspaper and reads.*) It says...(*Reading.*)...that the hostilities that have broken out in the enclave around Slavkov are as a direct result of a speech made by Herr Bonnke in Prague, the consequence of which was the recognition by Germany of the independence of the enclave.

LOLA: But why would he have got off the train if he knew there was a war on?

IMRI: To put your life at risk! In the hope that a stray bullet may kill you! And then he could live with my sister!

LOLA: (*Tearfully.*) No!

IMRI: It's obvious! Why would any man get off a train with his wife in a middle of a war unless he wanted her shot?

LOLA: It's not true! It's not!

IMRI: Of course it is! Not only that but he's known everything about the war ever since you arrived!

LOLA: But how could he?

IMRI: He goes out! He asks! He needs to keep track of Heinrich! God, can't you see? How could you be so blinded by love for a man who'd stick a gun in your mouth!

LOLA: Well if he knows all about the war then he'll know that they've taken the station and so he's risking his life for me by going there to find out the times of the trains so that we can leave!

IMRI: Stupid, foolish woman! Maybe he HASN'T gone there! Maybe he's gone to look for my sister! Maybe he's in the corridor!

LOLA: (*Hysterical.*) You're lying! You're lying! I don't know why you're lying! Get away from me! I've got my own life to lead even if it's not leading anywhere! I hate you! You think I'm blinded by the love I have for my husband? Why shouldn't I be? Why should it matter to you what he puts in my mouth? One day it might be a gun, one day something else! I'm going to look for him! I'm going to die with him at the station!

(*LOLA begins to get up.*

IMRI slaps her ferociously across the face.

LOLA falls back down onto bed.

IMRI holds LOLA's head to comfort her.

LOLA's head is on IMRI's belly.

BRECHT bursts on with gun.)

BRECHT: So!

(*LOLA gasps.*)

No sooner am I gone than you're at it! Get away from my wife you greaseball!

(*BRECHT has gun pointed at IMRI.*)

LOLA: What's the matter Peter? He's just comforting me.

BRECHT: If he's comforting you what the buggery were you doing to him? I don't know how you've got the balls to speak to me with a mouth that's just sucked his penis!

LOLA: Penis?! Peter, you're mad! Look! There's no penis here! Have a look!

BRECHT: Lola, shut up! I can smell it on your breath from here! (*To IMRI.*) Right you! No false moves! I'm going to close my eyes for three seconds. When I open them again I want it put away.

LOLA: But there's nothing to put away!

BRECHT: Shut up whore! (*Closes his eyes. No one moves.*) One thousand, two thousand, three thousand…(*To IMRI.*) Right. Over here.

LOLA: I thought you were at the station.

BRECHT: I changed my mind. Just as well I did!
(*IMRI goes to BRECHT.*)

BRECHT: (*To IMRI.*) On your knees.
(*IMRI falls to his knees.*
BRECHT stands behind him.)

LOLA: You didn't. You didn't go Peter. Imri was right.
(*BRECHT points gun at LOLA.*)

BRECHT: O, Imri is it? Very nice. Lola, open your mouth once more and I'll button it with a bullet!

LOLA: Peter!
(*BRECHT points gun at IMRI's head.*)

BRECHT: (*To IMRI.*) Okay, you…what are you? A Slav? What do you think you're doing putting your penis into my wife's mouth?

LOLA: He didn't! Leave him alone you bully!

BRECHT: (*Pointing gun at LOLA.*) Shut up! (*Gun back to IMRI.*) I'm asking you a question.

IMRI: You came here to feed off our suffering after starting our war. You said that if you could experience some of our suffering it would help you with your ministry!

BRECHT: I didn't tell you that!

IMRI: Nevertheless you said it!

BRECHT: So what?

IMRI: Don't you see? It's not possible for me to put my penis in your wife's mouth because I haven't got a penis!

BRECHT: (*Madly.*) What d'you mean you haven't got a penis? What do you piss through? Of course you've got a penis. And if you've got a penis and she's got her mouth open then one can go into the other!

IMRI: (*Angrily.*) No it's not! Because I am not a man! I am Imra!

BRECHT: Imra! Ha, ha, ha!

IMRI: (*Still angry.*) Not only that but I am not married to a German nor do I support the pro-German position of the enclave!

(*BRECHT pulls IMRA up. They look at each other face to face.*)

BRECHT: You've got a penis alright. It's all over your face! (*IMRA takes off her hat and lets her hair fall.*) That doesn't prove anything. Undo your trousers.

LOLA: Stop this Peter! Stop it! I'm looking at her! That's Imra! It's as if I've known all along!

BRECHT: (*Angrily.*) If that were the case, what would it all mean?!

LOLA: It would mean that she's been lying to you.

BRECHT: But why?

IMRA: Because you have to pay for Herr Bonnke's words! (*IMRA suddenly lets her trousers fall. There is a rifle shot. BRECHT is flung to the side, opposite from where LOLA is on the bed.*
IMRA rushes off.
Silence.)

BRECHT: (*With difficulty.*) I'm shot! (*LOLA cries. She's terrified.*)

LOLA: (*With difficulty.*) Are you hurt…badly?

BRECHT: I don't know. Can you come and look?

LOLA: I can't move.

BRECHT: Why?

LOLA: I'm paralysed.

BRECHT: Were you shot too?

LOLA: No. It's fear.

BRECHT: But Lola! I could be dying! You're a nurse! I NEED you to help me!

LOLA: I'm afraid you married a coward Peter.

BRECHT: O not now! Not now Lola!

LOLA: Not now what?

BRECHT: These complicated emotional arguments!
(*Silence.*)
I'm sorry, Lola, I'm sorry.

LOLA: I'll try.
(*LOLA gets up. She takes a few steps from the bed and comes into the line of fire.*
A shot rings out.
LOLA screams out and falls back onto bed.)

BRECHT: Are you hit?

LOLA: No!

BRECHT: Thank Christ!

LOLA: You know what this means? It means the bed is the safest place. We need to make the bed our base. In an emergency we can always get down behind it. There's also the pillows. And in the case of an unrestrained volley we could pull the mattress over us!

BRECHT: I'm bleeding Lola.

LOLA: Is it a lot?

BRECHT: I think it might be.

LOLA: We'll have to stop the bleeding. Some of the bed sheets would help.

BRECHT: Then the bed IS our base.

LOLA: You need to get over here Peter.

BRECHT: Clearly. (*Pause.*) I think the only way would be for me to make a dash.

LOLA: (*Worriedly.*) Are you sure you could do that?

BRECHT: I don't know. I'll see if I can stand first.
(*Slowly, carefully, BRECHT stands.*)

LOLA: (*Joyfully.*) You're up, Peter!

BRECHT: Yes! I'm up! I'm going to try…I'm going to try to get to you.

LOLA: O, if only you could! But be careful!

BRECHT: I'll take a deep breath.

LOLA: Yes.

(*BRECHT takes a very deep breath.*)

BRECHT: Here I come!

LOLA: Come on!

(*BRECHT runs about three steps with difficulty and a shot rings out. He falls back crying out.*)

LOLA: O, no! Get back! Get back! Drag yourself back quickly!

(*BRECHT drags himself back frantically.*)

LOLA: Hurry! Hurry! O, God, are you alright?

BRECHT: My leg! I've been shot in the leg!

LOLA: Is it bad?

BRECHT: I DON'T KNOW!

(*Pause.*)

LOLA: Peter! If I tie a knot into the end of a bed sheet – to give it weight – then I could throw it over to you, you could pick it up, stand up as steadily as you can then I would give the biggest possible tug and you could be jerked over here in a second.

BRECHT: Try it!

(*LOLA pulls a sheet from the bed. She begins to prepare it to tie a knot then she stops. Silence.*)

Lola? (*Pause.*) What is it?

LOLA: I'm sorry, Peter, I can't help it. I can smell that woman on the sheet. (*Pause.*) Did you hear me?

BRECHT: Yes.

LOLA: That Imra.

BRECHT: I don't want to talk about her now. Not now.

LOLA: I don't want to either but it's her smell! Woman of destiny.

BRECHT: What?

LOLA: That Imra! A woman of destiny.

BRECHT: Why d'you say that? You seem to have a thing about destiny.

LOLA: She was so determined to get us! To trap us into her scheme! People of destiny always do that! Think of how she pretended to be that Imri! (*Ties knot. As she ties knot.*)

Think of it! As soon as she drops her trousers, a shot is fired from across there! She set the whole thing up so carefully! It's Heinrich over there sniping. It must be! Who else would be so annoyed that she was showing us her private parts.

BRECHT: But Lola, it can't be!

LOLA: Why?

BRECHT: Because Heinrich is on the German side. She's not!

LOLA: Then she must have made Heinrich up!

BRECHT: Exactly!

LOLA: But if it's not Heinrich, who is it?

BRECHT: (*Excited.*) Why should it matter who it is?! She said she wanted me to pay for Bonnke's words!

LOLA: Yes?

BRECHT: Well, this means that she's against Bonnke! Imra is against Bonnke! Isn't that wonderful? As far as I'm concerned, anyone who is against Bonnke is for me!
(*Silence. LOLA finishes tying the knot.*)

LOLA: Are you ready?

BRECHT: We'll try.

LOLA: First of all I'll throw it to you.
(*LOLA gets up to throw the sheet. As soon as she lifts her arm to begin the swing, a shot rings out. LOLA screams. She falls back on the bed.*)

BRECHT: (*Panicking.*) Are you hit, Lola? Lola! Are you hit?!

LOLA: I think I'm nicked.

BRECHT: Where?

LOLA: On the back of my neck.

BRECHT: Are you?
(*LOLA feels.*)

LOLA: Yes, I am. O, no! O, no! I feel so scared!

BRECHT: Is it a serious nick?

LOLA: It's beginning to hurt a bit now so I suppose it is.

BRECHT: Shit! (*Pause.*) Wrap the sheet around your neck.

LOLA: No, it's alright.

BRECHT: Lola, do it!

LOLA: No!

BRECHT: Why not?

LOLA: Because then I'd virtually have that woman's smell up my nose! There could even be something left on the sheet that could go into my wound!

BRECHT: God, Lola! That's disgusting! Just ignore it? Please? It's not as if it meant anything to me.

LOLA: What do you mean?

BRECHT: Well...what happened with her. With that Imra.

LOLA: So you did do it? It did happen?

BRECHT: You know that! And I'm sorry Lola. I'm sorry. I can't think what came over me.

LOLA: By the smell of this she did!

BRECHT: Lola! Don't go on about it please! Not now! Not at a time like this!

(Silence.

LOLA puts the bed sheet to her neck.)

BRECHT: *(As if suddenly discovering something.)* Lola! The light! Why didn't I see it before?

LOLA: What?

BRECHT: Why didn't I think of it? We need to turn the light out! That's how he can see into the room! And it's not far to the light switch! You should just be able to reach it without being seen.

(Pause.)

LOLA: Actually, I think I could get quite close but I don't think I could actually switch it off without being seen. It'd mean taking a lunge.

BRECHT: Okay, then. Do it!

LOLA: I'll try. My neck's hurting.

BRECHT: You just need to put that light out then you can get over here and we can treat each other.

LOLA: Yes. *(Pause.)* You're right. *(Pause. LOLA wraps sheet around her neck.)* I'm going to wrap it round. Like you said. Around my neck. And I'm going to pretend the smell is you. And dream about you. Your sperm.

(Pause.)

BRECHT: Are you being ironic?

(*LOLA suddenly springs up and lunges for the light switch. She hits the switch. As the light goes out a shot rings out. She hits the floor.*)

(*In panic.*) Lola! Lola?

(*LOLA stands in the dark.*)

LOLA: I did it Peter! I did it! I'm standing bold as brass in the middle of the room in the middle of that sniper's line of fire and I'm alright!

BRECHT: Brilliant!

(*Suddenly a light floods into the room from outside. LOLA lets out a scream. She flings herself onto bed as shot rings out. LOLA lets out a cry.*)

Lola!

(*LOLA moans.*)

They've brought their own bloody lights! Lola! Are you alright? (*Pause.*) Lola?

LOLA: I've been shot.

BRECHT: O, God, no! Where?

LOLA: It doesn't matter.

BRECHT: It does! Where have you been shot?

LOLA: In the leg.

BRECHT: In the leg too? They must be trying to stop us from walking. To stop us from getting anywhere! And they've brought their own lighting! What kind of people are these?

LOLA: Murderers.

(*Silence.*)

BRECHT: Do you think you can move?

LOLA: I think so.

BRECHT: Where in the leg are you hit?

LOLA: Towards the top.

BRECHT: Not in a muscle?

LOLA: No.

BRECHT: In flesh?

LOLA: Yes.

BRECHT: Towards the top of the leg then?

LOLA: Why does it matter?

BRECHT: I want to know how badly hit you are!

LOLA: It's in my bum.

BRECHT: The bullet's in your bum?

LOLA: No. The shot is. The bullet...I think the bullet's gone.

BRECHT: How can you tell if the bullet's gone out of your bum?

LOLA: It doesn't matter! I've had enough! I can't feel anything any more!
(*Silence.*)

BRECHT: I'm going to ask you a big thing now, Lola. Maybe the biggest thing I'll ever ask you. And I'm taking into account the fact that you've been shot in your bum. In fact, I should think that the sheet is long enough to go round your neck and down your body where you could pull it between your legs and wrap it round your bum. (*Pause.*) Do you think you could get to the window? Do you? Can you get to the window and draw the curtains?

LOLA: O, God, Peter! If only I could!

BRECHT: (*Impatiently. With panic.*) But what do you mean? (*Pause.*) Lola? (*Silence.*) If you don't, we've got no future. There is NOTHING if you don't close the curtains!

LOLA: (*Tearfully.*) Don't you think I know that? Do you think I don't know that if I could close those curtains we could maybe get out of the door, get help and maybe even get to Prague? Get to a hospital?

BRECHT: So why are you humming and ha-ing? If you ever needed to get anywhere in your life EVER, you need to get to that bloody window!

LOLA: But who am I? Who am I to think I could do it? I think you need an Anne Frank to get to those curtains. A heroine. I've lost direction in life if I ever had it! I just don't think I've got the...courage.

BRECHT: Courage?! You, Lola?! It's absurd! Courage is your middle name! You are courage personified! You are the flesh of courage! My religion has come out of you! Christ's suffering is as nothing compared to what you've had to put up with. And let's be clear: I know just how responsible I've been for that suffering. And this latest despicable act...with that Imra...

LOLA: You seemed overjoyed when you said that she must be against Bonnke. She still means a lot to you doesn't she? (*Silence.*) Peter?

BRECHT: I may as well be honest with you, Lola, you deserve it.

LOLA: Thank you, Peter.

BRECHT: When I saw her I felt as if I'd fallen in love for the first time ever. (*Silence.*) Now I realise it was different! I love you in a different way!

LOLA: What way is that?

BRECHT: I love you for...for your nursing skills.

LOLA: Skills?

BRECHT: Yes.

LOLA: That's not very flattering.

BRECHT: No. But you know how to put a bandage on. I can't believe it even now! I can't believe I could have done it! But that's me isn't it? That's the depths I've sunk to. Blindness. It IS blindness. That's how I couldn't tell that that Imri was that Imra! I couldn't see it! Why couldn't I see it? Because I was blind! I AM blind! I've become blind. I was blind to that light till I noticed the switch on the wall! But I am getting it back! I'm getting my sight back! And now I can see. That's why I can see that we shouldn't concern ourselves even with Prague. We shouldn't give it a second thought. We should think only of getting to the window. To the curtains! If we could draw the curtains then...well, who knows? Anything is possible. Let's do it Lola! For God's sake...no, not for God's sake and certainly not for Bonnke's sake, for the sake of our, as yet unborn children, for the sake of doing something that might have untold consequences. Let's do it!

LOLA: (*Uplifted.*) That sounds so hopeful! So...O Peter! 'Our, as yet unborn, Children'! CHILDREN! (*Pause.*) I COULD get to the curtains! I could skirt around the room. Staying to the floor. I don't think that's a problem. The problem would be with getting them shut.

BRECHT: But if you skirt round the room then you can get to the bottom of the curtains and close them like that. From the bottom.

LOLA: I've thought of that. But I'm looking at them Peter and my limited experience of curtains…

BRECHT: Don't put yourself down!

LOLA: What?

BRECHT: You've got the widest experience of curtains of anyone I've ever known! You should celebrate your virtues! O, God, Lola! I can't believe I let myself think that that was Imri and that that Imri…raped you! And all that disgusting farrago of sexual accusations I made you suffer. All for destiny! And I wonder: do I really want a destiny after all?

LOLA: I think you're having one whether you want it or not.

BRECHT: O let's get out of here! Let's close those curtains! (*Pause.*)

LOLA: My worry about closing them from the bottom is, IF I try to close them from the bottom and they won't close that sniper will see the movement in the tugging and spray the room with bullets and you may get hit again.

BRECHT: Well I don't think he'll spray the room. Hardly. He's only got a rifle, not a machine gun. But I take your point. The trouble is you won't know. You won't know if they're those kind of curtains unless you get there. If you get there you'll be able to tell if they're the kind of curtains that will close from the bottom or not.

LOLA: What it's going to need is one swift definite action. To close them with one movement.

BRECHT: Do you think you could do it?

LOLA: I think I could. Just. Now, anyway. But what it'll mean is that if they won't close from the bottom, I'll have to stand full-bodied for a split second in the window and give both curtains one good tug.

BRECHT: Do it!

(*LOLA gets onto floor. She begins to crawl. As she crawls she speaks.*)

LOLA: I'm on my way Peter! To where our future lies!

BRECHT: You can do it! If anyone can do it, you can!

LOLA: It's not such a big thing! Not when you can do it for the one you love!

(*LOLA makes a lot of noise: grunting and groaning.*)

BRECHT: Aren't human beings such silly things?

LOLA: What do you mean?

BRECHT: Well, getting so worked up about Rheinardt Bonnke. Who is he? Hardly anyone! Ha, ha! And what a name! Bonnke! Bonnke! Ha, ha! You'd think that a man who had his toe on the threshold of destiny would have changed his name to something more appropriate! Something you could imagine seeing in the history books! Like me. Brecht! But Bonnke! Brechtian sounds right. Bonnkian! Bonnkist! Bonnkist values!...Bonnkism. Bonnkism like Buddhism! Ha, ha! BONNKism! Ha, ha! I'll never get worked up about Bonnke again you can be sure of that! You know, it's funny, I feel hardly any pain at all now! Only a little if I laugh. But then again I don't mind laughing at Bonnke's expense! And just think: could Bonnke survive something like this? Good God, no! You can somehow picture it can't you: me, Brecht lying in my own blood in a moment of history while Bonnke...well where is he? Totally OUT of the picture!

LOLA: (*With difficulty.*) When I get to you, I'll take this sheet off and rip it up to make bandages and tie you all up...

BRECHT: Nurse me.

LOLA: Nurse you! Yes! Like when we first met. When I was a nurse and you virtually ripped my clothes off that first night! Do you remember?

BRECHT: I'm feeling guilty now about the smell.

LOLA: What smell? Our first night smell?

BRECHT: Good God, no! No, the smell of that woman.

LOLA: Imra.

BRECHT: Yes.

LOLA: It's alright. By the time I get to you you'll only smell me I'm sweating so much!

BRECHT: God, Lola, you're quaint. What did I ever see in that pissing Slav, Gypsy... whatever she is?
(*LOLA is almost at the window.*)

LOLA: Bloody hell, this is an experience Peter! This is giving my life so much meaning! I can feel it surge up in me! Isn't it funny? You know, you were a bit right about Marthe – Marthe and me. I didn't tell you, of course, why should I? Why should you be interested...I'll just stop here and rest before the final push...You were on your way to fame and glory with that sermon you would have made...

BRECHT: (*Becoming weaker.*) I don't think so Lola...

LOLA: I hoped so!

BRECHT: You did?

LOLA: O yes. I tried to live my life by your sermons but then it all got me down. So I thought: let me answer Marthe's letter. I'll tell her that I am coming to Prague. I felt certain that in your time of glory in Prague, you would take much less notice of me – which is what I knew you wanted deep down, and I could slip off with Marthe. And I felt that things would probably have been better all round.

BRECHT: (*Weakly.*) I can't quite understand what you're saying, Lola.

LOLA: I'm saying I was going to Prague to leave you. For Marthe. Well not exactly 'for Marthe' – how could I know that. But we were once in love and she could have been a companion at least.

BRECHT: You mean...you were lesbians?

LOLA: If you want to call it that. But it's not just a lot of sex – which is what you might think. We cared for each other. (*Pause.*) I'd become desperate, Peter: I'd even thought I'd fallen in love with that Imri. (*Silence. Ready to jump up to curtains.*) Just think! This morning I was a woman who felt she could do almost nothing – someone sliding along in the slime of someone else's history and now here I am about to do T-H-I-I-I-I-I-SSSSSS!!!!!! (*As she stands in the light of the window there's a volley from a machine gun. LOLA flies back and falls on BRECHT.*) I did it!

BRECHT: A bloody machine gun! (*Silence. Weak.*) Lola! Lola? (*Pause.*) Next time we won't get off the train till we get to where we're going.

(*There is a shot. The sniper's light goes out. Darkness. BRECHT dies.*)

LOLA: Someone's shot the sniper's lights out! We can get out! (*Silence.*) Peter?

(*After a moment there is a knock on the door.*)

(*Weakly.*) Yes?

(*Another knock.*)

Who is it?

(*IMRA comes on. She switches light on.*)

IMRA: It's Imra. (*She goes to BRECHT. She bends over him.*) He's dead. (*Silence.*) Let me look at you. (*She looks at LOLA's wounds.*)

LOLA: Would you do me a favour?

IMRA: Yes?

LOLA: Could you make a phone call to Prague? To my friend Marthe? To let her know...to let her know that I've been delayed?

IMRA: Do you want to get to Prague?

LOLA: Yes.

IMRA: I can do that for you. (*She goes to phone and picks it up.*) What was the number?

Lights down.

The End.